THE TEENS SELF-REGULATION WORKBOOK

Empowering Teenagers to Understand, Handle and Master Their Emotions With Success Through CBT Exercises and Coping Strategies

By **Vivian Foster**

SOMETHING FOR YOU!

Get your printable workbook today!

Scan this code to download.

Table of Contents

Introduction

"It is a choice. No matter how frustrating or boring or constraining or painful or oppressive our experience, we can always choose how we respond." – **Edith Eger**

All throughout your tween years, you may have waited with bated breath until the day you became a teen. So many films, series, and comics make the teen years seem so cool. They immerse adolescents in a host of exciting adventures—whether it be experiencing new things with friends, feeling more independent, or getting ready for life as a college student. Nobody seems to talk about how hard it can be, though.

If you are having a tough time at school, or struggling in your relationships with friends, or family, know that despite its downside, these years may, indeed, be the most incredible time of your life. Ask any adult you love, and they will probably tell you that it was during their teen years that they made their best friends, made a host of mistakes, and learned some of the most important life lessons they still value today.

Being a teen today has many challenges, and whether you are a teen or a parent, it is vital to be aware of what these challenges are. Let's look at a few pertinent statistics:

- Americans aged 15-29 and 30-49 are the most stressed in the nation.

- Many teens are battling debilitating anxiety. In the US, anxiety and depression affect up to 70 percent of teens.[1]

---

[1] Child Welfare League of America, n.d.

- The most common stress triggers for teens are:[2]

  - school (83 percent)

  - getting into a good college or deciding what to do with their lives (69 percent)

  - financial problems in their family (65 percent)

- Around 35 percent of teens lie awake at night, 26 percent overeat or eat unhealthy foods, and 23 percent skip meals because of stress.

- Teens say that during the school year, their average stress level is 5.8 out of 10, compared to 4.6 during the summer.

- Over one-quarter of teens have snapped at classmates or teammates when stressed, and 51 percent say that someone has told them they looked stressed at least once a month.

---

[2] Smith, 2022.

Cause of Anger

There are five main causes for anger in teens:

A wish for more self-reliance and independence.
Puberty (mood swings, hormonal surges, brain development, etc)
Stress (academic, family, and social).
Medical conditions such as ADHD and bipolar disorders.
Substance abuse.

If you are a teen, you may feel pulled in many directions. Your parents may expect you to get high grades, excel at sports, or work hard so that a talent you have (like singing, dancing, or playing sports) can one day be your career.

Yet at this point in your life, you'd like to hang out more with your friends—in fact, friendships can take on much greater importance than when you were a tween. Friendships, however, can also be a source of worry. You want to be perceived as a cool kid, yet you want to be yourself. You would love to get on with everyone but sometimes find it hard to control emotions like boredom, irritation, or anger.

For some kids, everything seems to come so easily—grades, friends, relationships with teachers. You may sometimes find it hard to communicate with classmates and teachers, feel shy when you are asked to present a project in class, or find it almost impossible to stop chatting in class—even after your teacher has specifically asked you to focus.

If you are a parent, you may be at a loss, and for the first time in your child's life, you may be questioning your parenting style. You know how competitive the world is, and you want your teen to hone all the skills they need to excel. Yet sometimes, you wish you could just wrap your child in your arms and shelter them from all the pressures and pains of teen life. You sometimes have to hold back from expecting too much from your teen, and you may recall the wise words of John Lennon: "When I went to school, they asked me what I wanted to be when I grew up. I wrote down, 'Happy.' They told me I didn't understand the assignment, and I told them they didn't understand life."

You may keep your worry and stress about the future deep inside, but know that you are not alone. There are important reasons why teens find this time in life so stressful, and much of it has to do with the fact that their brains are still in the process of maturation.

If you are a teen reader who wishes they could nip stress and anxiety in the bud, control your anger, and battle shyness or social anxiety, know that it is possible to do so if you build emotional regulation skills. I am here to make it easier through a series of practical exercises and worksheets that will help you know more about the sometimes complex world of emotions.

I also want you to learn more about yourself and the vital link between the way you think, feel, and act. Through greater understanding, you can manage difficult emotions and feel more in control of your own life. This, in turn, can make you feel more confident in a variety of settings—including the classroom, your home, and social occasions with friends.

You may not have heard of "cognitive-behavioral therapy" before. Also known as "CBT," it is not as complex as it may sound! CBT is the top treatment of choice that therapists use to help people with conditions like anxiety, depression, and difficulties managing their anger. It works by getting people to understand how negative thinking or negative self-belief can lead them to behave in unproductive ways. It highlights the importance of reframing negative thoughts and emotions to more positive ones, so you can make rational, smart decisions that can have a huge impact on your school, social, and family life.

I have written various books on subjects such as ADHD, Anger management, Life skills and Social skills and one therapy that is often recommended for a plethora of mental health issues is CBT. This therapy is considered one of the very best for adults as well as teens because it tackles problems from many angles. It shows that you can change your behavior by changing the way you think, but it also works the other way around. By changing unproductive behavior, you can also change the way you think or feel about a situation or person. CBT has been one of my strongest passions during my 20-year study of Psychology, and I am ready to bring you the most important lessons I have learned and experienced.

Thankfully, mental health is no longer the taboo subject it once was. Many young stars—including Justin Bieber, Lili Reinhart, and Sophie Turner—have told the world that their adolescence was far from easy. Many have praised CBT and other therapies, highlighting the perspective and calm it has brought to their lives.[3]

By the time you have finished reading this book and completed some of over 105 CBT activities and worksheets, you will know yourself better and be able to live in a way that is much truer to your values and beliefs. My aim isn't to drown you in theoretical concepts or bore you with endless explanations but, rather, to highlight the power of CBT through true stories and practical exercises. You don't have to do all the exercises; just pick and choose those you find most effective. From the very first chapter onwards, you will start understanding the important role you play in your own happiness, independence, and maturity. Have fun with the exercises and stay committed you will discover more about yourself than you ever imagined!

---

[3] Valenti, 2019.

Part 1

CBT

For

Emotional Regulation

Chapter One

Emotional Regulation Can Be Tough for Teens

"The biggest challenge to self-control is emotional regulation. Successful people know how to make their emotions servants rather than masters." – **Paul TP Wong**

Sam's Story

My daughter, Claire's best friend, let's call her Sam (not her real name), struggled through high school because she had difficulty expressing her feelings. When she was annoyed with someone, she found it hard to let them know why, fearing she would hurt them if she told them how she felt about them, and trying to avoid the unpleasant side of confrontations. She would keep things in and allow them to simmer and bubble.

Suddenly, a friend might say something slightly triggering one day and Sam would disconnect, ghosting the friend for a few weeks. When she had cooled down, she would start talking to the friend again, as if nothing had ever happened between them. There was only one problem: her friends got tired of being ignored and ghosted. Ghosting hurts—for many, more so than an outburst. Sam needed to learn how to communicate better with her friends, but in order to do so, she needed to regulate her emotions, so she could speak to them assertively and respectfully, without losing her cool.

Why Are Emotions So Hard to Regulate?

Emotional regulation is tough—not only for teens but also for many adults. There are various reasons why, in tense situations, it can be hard to identify, let alone manage your emotions. These reasons include:

The "Fight or Flight" Response

When you perceive a situation as stressful or frightening, your body goes into "fight or flight" mode. To understand how this response works, imagine you are in a jungle and see a wild animal. In the face of danger, a chain of events is brought about, so you can either defend yourself against the animal (fight) or flee to safety (flight). Your heart rate increases, blood is shunted to the skeletal muscles and brain, your bronchi dilate, and you begin to breathe faster. There is an increased availability of oxygen in the blood, your skin becomes flushed, and your pupils dilate.[4]

All these responses can play a critical role in helping you survive when you are in a situation of real danger. When you have anxiety, however, your "threat system" can become overactive, and you can go into "fight or flight" mode even when you are not in any danger at all. For instance, a discussion with a friend, an upcoming exam, or fear about having to speak before your class can trigger a panic attack. Even after the fearful moment has passed, your body has to deal with the stress that has been created, and it is important to know how to deal with and curb this stress.

---

[4] Psychology Tools, n.d.

Your Brain Is Still Maturing

The teen years are a time of significant growth for the teenage brain. The main change that occurs during adolescence is that unused connections in the thinking and processing part of your brain (gray matter) are pruned away while other connections are strengthened. As such, your brain is becoming more and more efficient every day!

This pruning process starts at the back of the brain. The front part of the brain (called the "prefrontal cortex") is remodeled last. The prefrontal cortex is used to make decisions, plan and think about the consequences of your actions, and control your impulses. As it is still in the process of maturing, it can be much harder to keep your emotions in check.[5]

Hormonal Changes in the Teen Years

Teenage hormones are the chemicals that cause the physical growth and development that carry you into adulthood. The surge in hormones you experience can affect your mood, make you feel more impulsive, and make you more inclined to take risks.

Hormonal changes can also alter your behavior. When combined with peer pressure, low self-esteem, and other problems that can arise, they can lead you to behave in unproductive ways.[6]

Chronic Stress and Trauma

Not all teens have been through stressful or traumatic childhoods, but those who have can find it harder to regulate their emotions. Trauma

---

[5] Raising Children, n.d.
[6] Newport Academy, 2022.

from abuse can make you more "reactive" and make you less tolerant of stressful situations.

Being "reactive" means that you react to situations through your emotions. When you are reactive, you tend to blame others for your choices and can come across as resentful or angry.[7] Examples of statements you might make when you are being reactive include:

- "She ruined my day."
- "The teacher was being unfair."
- "I can't do anything to change this."
- "It's just the way I am; I can't change it."
- "They make me so mad."
- "I must … I can't … I have to …If only …"

There is a much more productive way to deal with challenging situations and circumstances: being proactive. This means taking ownership of your actions and choices and using them to learn and grow. It means being authentic with others. For instance, if someone doesn't understand your point of view, you recognize that you may need to communicate more clearly. If a conflict arises, you look forward to resolving it and preventing it from happening in the future. When you are proactive, you might say:[8]

- "Let's look at some alternatives."
- "I control how I react to my feelings."
- "I choose… I prefer… I will."
- "I can try a different approach."

---

[7] Resolve, n.d.
[8] Central Washington University, n.d.

What Are Some of the Toughest Emotions for Teens to Handle?

Some of the emotions and states teens find hardest to handle include:

- stress/anxiety
- anger
- sadness
- loneliness
- jealousy
- self-Criticism
- rejection
- fear

Teens and Depersonalization

Teens can sometimes feel detached from their own lives as if they are living in a dream. Sometimes, this is the result of traumatic events or experiences. It is as if the brain "shuts off," so you no longer feel pain.[9] This can lead you to feel isolated and make it hard to feel good emotions when people are trying to provide comfort. If depersonalization is the result of trauma, seeking help from a therapist is vital, as it will enable you to feel more emotion and regain a positive view of the world and the people around you.

The Key Steps to Emotional Regulation

What does regulating your emotions involve?

When you regulate your emotions effectively, you:[10]

---

[9] Paradigm Treatment, n.d.
[10] Newport Academy, 2022.

Know how to Identify Your Emotions

The first step in emotional regulation is to identify the bodily sensations and thoughts that indicate you are feeling a certain way. For instance, if you are angry, you may notice that your face gets flushed, your ears get red, you start breathing faster, and your fists clench. You can say to yourself, "I'm angry right now." Acknowledge the emotion and don't fight it, but don't let it take control over your behaviors, either.

Identify Emotions in Others

You can read others' body language and tone of voice. For instance, if you are talking about something with a friend, and they are huffing and puffing, looking away, or rolling their eyes, you can appreciate that they are getting annoyed. These are signals that you need to make them feel understood or lower the tension of the moment if you want your talk to be productive. They are also signs that it might be better to take a small break and reconnect a bit later in the day or even the following day.

Understand the Expectations of Your Social Environment

When you regulate your emotions well, you know that it is not acceptable, for instance, to yell in class or a restaurant, bang your desk, or display emotions aggressively. You know how to be respectful, even if the person across from you is not behaving as you would like.

Know how to Express or Keep Emotions in Check to Support Your Goals

When someone refuses to cooperate or uses aggressive body or verbal language, it is very hard to "keep it together" and be mindful of your goal. You may have to reach a compromise with this person. If you lose your cool, you may never come to an agreement at all, and that means that you may not achieve what you need to.

Emotional regulation does not mean ending tough conversations and stonewalling someone else. In fact, maturity involves having important conversations—even difficult ones. Of course, you can take a break if the situation is tense, but it is important to get back to it and resolve your conflict instead of ghosting someone and then talking to them a few days later as if "nothing has happened." When you ghost people this way, nothing gets resolved.

Start and Persist on Long-term Goals, Even When You Feel Anxious

There are many times during your teen years that you can feel stressed—for instance, you may have an upcoming driver's exam or an important project to present in class. Emotional regulation involves continuing to forge ahead so you achieve these goals, even when they make you tense.

Problem-solve to Achieve Goals

You may have a part-time job while you are at school, and you may have to sort through various challenges in your interactions with others. As problems arise in each of these areas, you know how to think up possible solutions, choose the solution you think is best, and assess how your strategy works. If the strategy did not produce the outcome you expected, you try another strategy next time.

The Ability to Resist Peer Pressure if It Is Negative

Peer pressure can be positive—for instance, if everyone in your friend group works out and you, too, start hitting the gym, this is a positive thing for your physical and mental health. However, peer pressure can also steer you in the wrong direction—for instance, when your friends disrespect a teacher, bully others, or suggest cutting class. It is vital to be confident in saying "no" when someone is trying to get you to do something you don't want to or something that is inappropriate for your age.

The Ability to Soothe Your Own Emotions

You can do so by reframing negative thoughts (which we learn all about in Chapter 2), saying positive affirmations to yourself, practicing belly breathing, meditating, exercising, and so many more self-soothing activities.

Belly Breathing

This exercise is easy to perform but ultra-effective. Belly breathing lowers your heart rate almost immediately, and is very efficient at stopping anxiety in its tracks. Follow these steps and you will have a powerfully ally that will stand you in good stead during tense moments (Gotter, 2019):

1. Sit or lie down in a quiet spot.

2. Put one hand under your rib cage and one hand on your chest.

3. Inhale through your nose for around four seconds, noticing how your belly expands.

4. Hold your breath for around two seconds.

5. Exhale through your nose or mouth for about six seconds, noticing how your belly goes back to its normal position.

The Ability to Soothe Others

You may find your friends feeling sad, tense, angry, or anxious. Emotional regulation involves knowing the right things to say to them so they feel a little better.

The Ability to Delay Gratification

When you are impulsive, you seek short-term rewards. However, by keeping your mind on immediate rewards, your goals and relationships can suffer. It pays to think of the long-term effects of your actions. Sometimes, it is better to sacrifice feeling good "in the moment" inorder to achieve goals and have healthy relationships with others.

Self-monitor and Self-reward When You Are Pursuing Goals

When you are working on something that is goal-oriented, it is vital to check on your progress and reward yourself every time you achieve a goal. Doing so will make you feel more motivated to work towards new achievements.

1. Making decisions with a broad perspective and compassion for self and others. It's always important to see "the bigger picture" when you make a decision, and you must analyze how it might affect others, not just yourself.

2. Seeking help when stress is unmanageable or if the situation is dangerous. Help can come in the form of a loving family member or friend, but if your stress is taking over your life, then professional therapy may be indicated.

How Can Emotional Regulation Benefit You?

When you manage your emotions, you can enjoy a myriad of benefits.[11] These include:

---

[11] Murray & Rosanbalm, 2017.

- Improved conflict resolution: Conflict resolution simply refers to finding a positive way to deal with conflicts and disagreements you have with others. Conflicts are not always negative. In fact, they can play an important role in strengthening relationships since they provide an opportunity for you and others to make meaningful changes in your relationship.

- Better stress management: When you know your emotions well, you can take steps early to keep stress levels down. In fact, you may notice that during stressful times, it can make a big difference if you exercise, sleep well, and eat healthily. When you know you are feeling low, you also know that it is time to seek support from friends and family.

- An ability to cope with anger: Anger is another emotion that can produce positive change when you deal with it productively. You can stop anger from gaining control and use it to set boundaries (let people know what you are comfortable or uncomfortable with). When you have healthy boundaries, it is easier to say no, especially when someone is asking you to do something you are uncomfortable with or you feel you should not be doing.

- Becoming more resilient: Resilience is the ability to bounce back quickly from difficulties. When you experience a stressful situation but can take the reins of your thoughts and emotions, it is easier to "spring back into shape" instead of falling to pieces.[12]

- Enjoying better physical and mental health: We mentioned how stress could harm your short and long-term health. Keep stress in check, and you are likely to feel good mentally and physically.

---

[12] Hurley, 2022.

- Having a better academic performance: How often have you had to work on group projects with classmates? It may not have been easy (since everyone has their own personality and everyone may have a different idea of how to go about a project). Keeping your emotions in check enables you to be more tolerant of others and to keep your eye on the end goal. Use your emotional intelligence to steer others towards this goal instead of bickering over things like who does what and who gets to do the most entertaining part of the project. Aim to enlighten others on the importance of sharing tasks and responsibilities.

- Richer personal relationships: You probably know someone you consider to be "emotionally together." They know how to keep it cool and think about others as well as themselves, yet they are no pushover. They live by their values and ensure their boundaries are respected. Know that they are this way simply because they have honed skills that anyone can use to their benefit—including you!

Emotional regulation helps you be your best self, and the result is that both you and others reap important rewards.

What is Cognitive-Behavioral Therapy (CBT)?

This book is, in part, a workbook containing CBT exercises. We spoke earlier about how your thoughts, emotions, and behaviors are intertwined. CBT encourages you to stop negative thoughts from resulting in emotions that are difficult to control—which in turn result in unwanted behaviors.

Understanding the Difference Between Thoughts, Feelings, and Behaviors/Actions

1. Thoughts are words that run through your mind. They are the things you tell yourself about what is occurring around you.

2. Emotions come and go as different things occur. They include happiness, sadness, frustration, anger, and joy.

3. Actions or behavior are the things you do. If you feel angry, frustrated, or sad, and you don't keep your emotions in check, you may behave in a way you regret or in a way that stands in the way of your goals.

The Basic Model of CBT

This model looks like a triangle.

You have probably noticed that there are two-sided arrows connecting THOUGHTS, BEHAVIORS, and EMOTIONS. The idea is that each of these three components of the CBT model affects the other.

For instance, your thoughts affect how you feel and act, but your feelings can also influence how you think and act. Your behaviors, meanwhile, can change the way you feel or think about things. Do you see how everything is interrelated?

More importantly, can you see how making positive changes to your thoughts, emotions, or behaviors can help you think and feel better about life and behave more productively?

The Basic Model of CBT

The three elements of the CBT model are supposed to interact with one another. For instance, your emotions might affect how you think and act, but your thoughts can also be influenced by your feelings. Your actions, however, have the power to affect your feelings and thoughts.

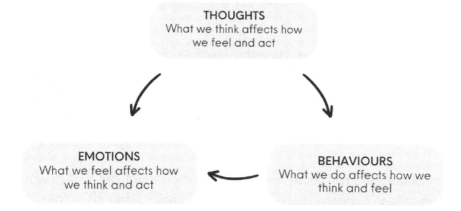

THOUGHTS
What we think affects how
we feel and act

EMOTIONS
What we feel affects how
we think and act

BEHAVIOURS
What we do affects how we
think and feel

A Few Examples of How the CBT Model Works[13]

1. You see a dog that is growling. You think, *It's going to bite me* (thought). You feel intense fear (emotion), and you run away (behavior).

2. You see a friend and don't say hello to her (behavior). You then feel guilty about it (emotion). You start to think that she won't speak to you tomorrow (thought).

3. You're feeling stressed (emotion), so you are short with a classmate who asks you a question (behavior). You then wonder

---

[13] Child Development Center, 2021.

if they are going to mention your rude behavior to other classmates (thought).

Exercises to Challenge Negative Thoughts

These exercises can help you view things in a more positive light and reframe negative thoughts into more positive ones.

Exercise One: Imaginary Thought, Emotion, Behavior

For the above examples, think of how changing the thought, behavior, or emotion could have led to a different outcome. What do you think would be the new outcome? For example:

For Example 1: You could think, *That dog is growling, but if I stay where I am, it won't approach me* (thought). You feel calmer (emotion), and you stay there (behavior).

For Example 2: You could think, *Even if I am tired, I will make it a point to say "Hello" to all my friends as they could feel hurt if I don't* (thought). You say hello to your friend (behavior), and you feel happy (emotion).

For Example 3: You might think, *I will deal with my stress* (thought). You breathe or head to a natural area until you are calmer (behavior). As a result, you are in a better mood (emotion).

Exercise Two: Choosing New Thoughts, Emotions, and Behaviors

Complete the following table the next time you face a tough or tense situation. It will help you view the world with a more positive lens. I have provided an example, so you can get the hang of how to complete the table:

Choosing New Thoughts, Emotions, and Behaviors

What happened?	I went to Emma's desk to have a chat and she raised her voice, saying she was too busy to chat. She got up angrily and went to the restroom.
What were my thoughts?	"She's so rude. Whenever she wants to talk I have to be ready, but when she's busy the world has to stop."
How did I feel?	"I'm boiling inside. How dare she get up and leave that way? It makes me feel angry, unappreciated, and despondent."
What did I do?	I waited until she was back and told her she was rude and not to count on me again when she felt like chatting.
New Thought	Emma is very busy today. It's best for me to return at another time. I know she sometimes interrupts me, but maybe I can talk to her about it tomorrow.
New Emotions	I'm concerned that Emma seemed annoyed with me, but I understand she must be snowed under with schoolwork and must be having a hard time fitting in all her schoolwork and extra-curricular activities. This makes me feel a lot calmer.
New Actions	I go back to my desk and talk to Emma the next day. I ask her if she was busy the day before, and she says she is sorry for being short. She explains that she is facing a lot of pressure to get better grades. I explain it is a little painful when she seems annoyed with me and tell her that if she tells me "I'm super busy" in a nice way, I will feel a lot better.
The Outcome	Emma and I understand how to communicate with each other better. The following week, when she is less busy, we spend time together and laugh and have a great time as we usually do.

Now your turn! To start, think of the time when you last faced a tough or tense situation? What happened? Continue by filling out the table.

YOUR TURN!
Fill in the table below.

What happened?	
What were my thoughts?	
How did I feel?	
What did I do?	
New Thought	
New Emotions	
New Actions	
The Outcome	

Exercise Three: The Plutchik Wheel Game

Print out a copy of Plutchik's Wheel, which is widely available online. This is a colorful wheel of emotions, which was created by psychologist Robert Plutchik.[14] The wheel shows that there are eight main emotions:

1. joy
2. trust
3. fear
4. surprise
5. sadness
6. disgust
7. anger
8. anticipation

Each of these emotions has a more and less intense version. The less intense version of joy, for instance, is serenity. Its more intense version is ecstasy. As such, the wheel has 24 emotions in total.

The Plutchik Wheel Game

The aim of this game is to get you used to differentiating between different emotions so you can recognize these emotions when you are feeling them.

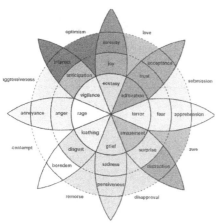

For the activity, take the wheel and cut it into the 24 emotions that make it up. Stick the emotions in a bag and invite friends or family members to play the game. Pull out an emotion and describe a situation that would likely produce that emotion in you. For instance, if you pick "serenity" you might say that being on the beach or going for a walk in the mountains makes you feel calm and serene. On the other hand, you may pick grief. This is an emotion you may have felt when a pet passed away.

---

[14] Child Development Center, 2021.

Exercise Four: Analyzing Difficult Emotions from the Past and Their Effect On Your Life Today

This exercise focuses on obtaining clarity about the past, so you can understand why certain emotions have such a strong effect on you today. This way, you can gain power over your thoughts and emotions. Think about a major event that happened in your life in the recent or distant past. It could be that your parents had a divorce, you moved to a new town, or your best friend decided to stop hanging out with you. I have provided an example table to inspire you.

The Situation: My parents separated

	Before the Situation	After the Situation
How did you feel...	Secure and happy.	Insecure, guilty, angry at my parents.
What things did you enjoy doing...	Spending time together as a family, doing sport with my parents on the beach, going to beach clean-ups.	Doing sport at school, playing video games, making TikTok videos, going to beach clean-ups.
What qualities did you look for in people...	I enjoyed friends with whom I shared interests.	I still hang out with friends that share my interest, but also look for friends who know how to listen.

YOUR TURN!

The Situation: _____

	Before the Situation	After the Situation
How did you feel...		
What things did you enjoy doing...		
What qualities did you look for in people...		

Exercise Five: Capture Your Memories

Write down some of the most important memories in your life. Describe the situation, your thoughts, and your emotions. Get back to this table in a few weeks and analyze whether you still feel that way when similar situations arise today.

SITUATION	THOUGHTS	EMOTIONS
I completed a mini-marathon.	I thought that this was an amazing achievement because it took me so much work.	I felt on top of the world.
My best friend moved schools.	I thought I would never again connect with a friend that deeply.	I felt sad, worried, and lonely.

Think of at least 3 events that happened in your life that you can't forget. Pick one event from school, one that happened at home, one that happened in a public place such as a mall, restaurant, park, etc. Create your own table (or use the printable version).

YOUR TURN!

SITUATION	THOUGHTS	EMOTIONS

Exercise Six: Grounding Technique

This exercise helps battle desensitization by making you more aware of what is going on around you. It boosts mindfulness, so you can simply "be" in the present moment without thinking about the past or future. I have filled in my set of answers. What are yours?[15]

Grounding Technique

Name five things you can see right now	I can see the sea from my window, the heater (which keeps me warm), a picture of my dog, a pair of spare glasses, and my ring.
Name four things you can feel	I feel the softness of my coat, the joy of my dog being near me, the warmth of the heater, and the worry of having to finish my project in time.
Name three things you can hear	I can hear my dog smacking her lips, and cars passing by in the distance.
Name two things you can smell	I can smell my perfume and the yummy lasagna I am eating as I write this.
Name one thing you can taste	I can taste the creamy bechamel sauce and the delicious minced beef in my lasagna.

[15] Therapist Aid, n.d.

YOUR TURN!

Name five things you can see right now	
Name four things you can feel	
Name three things you can hear	
Name two things you can smell	
Name one thing you can taste	

Returning to Sam

As the years went by, Sam found that she had trouble keeping friends. She would meet someone, create a strong bond with them, then seem to find something horrible about their personality that she did not talk to them about. She would then cut with this new friend, finding solace in her sisters and one or two friends she had had since she was a child (my daughter being one of them).

Claire continues to stay loyal to Sam but admits that it can be very hard to deal with her when she decides to "ghost" her. When Sam disappears, Claire simply lets her have her time, and when things have cooled down, she tries to see Sam in person to talk about what had happened.

Claire admitted to me that she was tired of this. As she has moved away from home and met many new people in college, she feels that Sam's way of dealing with things is toxic.

When you ghost others, shut them off, and simply return when you're ready with no explanation, it is easy for them to feel like the friendship is not equal. Everyone wants to have balance in their friendships. For friendships to stand the test of time and the many changes that take place in our lives, talking about conflict is essential. You can truly say almost anything you want or need to, so long as you are respectful and use proper conflict resolution skills.

Sam, if you are reading this, know that your friends are interested in what you have to say. They love you and are willing to change things that hurt you—but they can't change if they don't know what they did wrong in the first place. When you are in a conflict, you can keep things friendly by:

- Using "I" language. Talk about how someone makes you feel instead of what they do wrong. For instance, Sam could have said things like, "When you cut our conversation short because someone else is calling you, I feel like I matter less."

- Avoid using "You always" or "You never" when you are trying to fix an issue with friends. This makes them defensive, and they stop listening to you.

- Work as a team. If you and a friend have an issue, focus on the issue and how you can fix it instead of focusing on how "bad," "selfish," or "awful" your friend is. Commit to working together to find a solution that works relatively well for both of you. It's called compromise, and you will often need this quality if you want to maintain good friendships.

By now, you probably have a much greater understanding of what CBT is. You may be excited about completing more exercises and discovering more about yourself and the fascinating world of emotions. In Chapter Two, we will focus on the "cognitive" part of CBT. We will discover how to counter negative thoughts so that our emotions and behaviors can be more positive.

Chapter Two

Challenging Negative Thoughts

"Negativity is the enemy of creativity." – **David Lynch**

Tim's Story

Tim is a 16-year-old high school student who often struggled with his self-worth. When he was a child, he was subjected to frequent criticism and little praise. He had a sibling, Lars, who was five years older than him and who frequently preyed on Tim's sensitivity. Lars would call Tim "dumb," not allow his little brother to wear certain colors (because they were "his), and make fun of Tim when his friends were over. It didn't help that Lars was a straight-A student, played on the football team, and was super popular. Lars would also intimidate Tim physically, tripping him or throwing a wet towel on his face while he was studying.

Tim's mom and dad were kinder to him than Lars, but they had high expectations for him. Tim got little praise when he did things well; his parents never seemed to care too much when his report card was full of A-grades. However, if he was working on a coloring book and he colored slightly out of line, his mistakes were quickly pointed out to him.

Unlike Lars, Tim was not very athletic. He was a little scared of ball sports like basketball, as he feared being hit by the ball. Tim struggled with his weight, and his parents often put him on strict diets.

Tim's Story Cont.

The combination of factors Tim faced at home led him to engage in patterns of negative thinking. When he achieved good things (a good grade, a compliment from a teacher for doing well, making the swim team), he gave them little thought. However, he focused intensely on negative things and experiences—like getting a low grade on a test, missing a play during football, or receiving a critical comment from a classmate about something he was wearing. As a result, there were few moments in which he felt happy and fulfilled. He would overthink the bad things people had said and done in his head, yet never reward himself or feel grateful for all the good things that had happened.

Are Human Beings Naturally Negative?

Tim's experience is not unique; in fact, his negative view of the world is far more common than you may realize. As stated by education writer Linda Stade, "Human beings are naturally negative."[16] It's all got to do with evolution. In the early days of humanity, there were many natural threats in the environment (including the wild beasts that set off our fight-or-flight response). We, therefore, became more clued into negative details. Psychologists call this the *negativity bias*.

Modern threats no longer come in the form of saber-toothed tigers or mastodons. Our greatest perceived threats come in the form of people, relationships, and emotions. To protect ourselves:

---

[16] Linda State, n.d.

1. We sometimes look for negative qualities in people. Sometimes, when you meet someone new, you may be scared to let them into your circle, trust them, or even classify them as "cool." This might be because you are afraid, they will let you down, betray your trust, or not stick around the way good friends do. Research shows that when human beings meet new people, they tend to attribute negative motives to others more than positive ones. This negative view can (and often does) change when you get to know someone, but in the beginning, it's common to use filters or shields to protect yourself against hurt.

2. We can experience negative emotions more powerfully than positive ones. You may have found that it is much easier to hold on to pain and disappointment than to positive emotions like joy. For instance, you may have won your basketball game, got the phone number of someone you would love to get to know better, and aced your science project. However, a friend may have said something sarcastic to you instead of congratulating you, and just like that, your perfect day may have transformed into a bad one. It felt so painful that a friend would be spiteful instead of happy for you that you wondered how they could be so mean.

3. The closer you get to negative experiences, the more intensely negative they become, while the same is not true for positive events. For instance, if you are afraid of going to the dentist, your fear may grow far more quickly than the excitement or anticipation of having a sleepover that you were looking forward to on the weekend.

You can easily see how the above examples are ways of protecting yourself against danger. However, just because human beings evolved to view things negatively does not mean they must continue to do so. There is a myriad of ways to be more positive. These include:[17]

1. Being grateful for things. Try to think of the many good things that happened to you today. Write them down so you remember that life has many beautiful things.

2. Find something to look forward to every day. Research has shown that doing so boosts your mood and lowers stress.

3. Practice mindfulness. Aim to keep your mind in the present moment and give yourself fully to the people you are with. Try to avoid letting your mind get stuck in guilt or regret about the past or worry about the future.

4. Smile and laugh. Doing so releases feel-good chemicals in your brain that make you feel happier and more relaxed.

5. Use positive self-talk. Avoid self-criticism and remind yourself of all you have already achieved so you feel more confident about the goals and tasks ahead of you.

---

[17] Cherry, 2022.

Keep this in mind

When you are in a positive frame of mind, you...	When you are in a negative frame of mind, you...
Feel optimistic about the future.	Feel pessimistic about the future.
Are grateful.	Are ungrateful.
Look for solutions.	Focus on the problem.
Try to help others.	Do not try to help others.
Show empathy and compassion towards others.	Show little empathy or compassion for others.
Use humor to defuse tense situations.	Use cynicism or sarcasm.
Are upbeat.	Are in a bad mood.

How Do Negative Thoughts Affect You?

Thinking negative thoughts:[18]

- makes you feel bad about yourself and the world around you
- contributes to low self-worth
- makes you feel that you aren't contributing anything to the world
- is linked to anxiety, depression, chronic worry, OCD, and other health conditions
- saps your energy

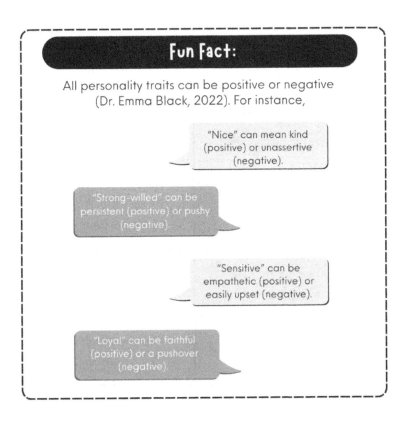

Fun Fact:

All personality traits can be positive or negative (Dr. Emma Black, 2022). For instance,

"Nice" can mean kind (positive) or unassertive (negative).

"Strong-willed" can be persistent (positive) or pushy (negative).

"Sensitive" can be empathetic (positive) or easily upset (negative).

"Loyal" can be faithful (positive) or a pushover (negative).

---

[18] Silber, 2021.

Cognitive Distortions: The Thoughts that Defeat Your Purpose

It is normal to trust your thoughts. Your brain is wired to protect you against danger, find solutions to problems, and attract you to people who are good for you. However, sometimes, you may want to question what your brain is telling you. Your brain can make unhelpful connections that can be harmful to you. Sometimes, however, there is no real connection between these situations or circumstances and finding one can be detrimental to your health and happiness. Something might just be a coincidence, or it could be far more complex than it seems at first. As such, it is important not to jump to conclusions.

What Are Cognitive Distortions?

Cognitive distortion involves taking a biased view of yourself and the world around you. It happens when you allow irrational thoughts and beliefs to take over a situation or your daily thoughts. When you use a distorted filter regularly, it becomes hard to make positive changes. This is because you may not realize you have to change anything at all.[19] Often, negative feelings are based on thinking errors.

What Do Cognitive Distortions Have in Common?

All cognitive distortions are:

- patterns or tendencies in thoughts or beliefs
- false
- capable of causing psychological harm

---

[19] Ackerman, 2017.

The Most Common Cognitive Distortions

Below is the list of the most common cognitive distortions or "thinking errors" that human beings can engage in:[20]

All-or-Nothing Thinking: Thinking that something is "all good" or "all bad" without acknowledging that there are often shades of gray.

Examples:

- You thought your friend was "the perfect BFF" until they let you down one day, canceling a plan at the last minute. Now you can't stand them.

- You always get As, but you get a C one day. Now, you see yourself as a bad student since you fail to take into account that you usually get top grades.

Overgeneralization: This thinking error happens when you take an isolated event and turn it into a continuous pattern of negativity.

Examples:

- Your friend arrived late twice this month. You say, "You always show up late. You never take my feelings into account."

- You are having a pretty good day, but someone steals your purse. You think thoughts like, *Everything bad happens to me* or *Nothing good happens to me*.

---

[20] Silva Casabianca, 2022.

Mental Filter: This refers to filtering out the good sides of a situation and sticking to the bad.

Examples:

- You did well on a test but got a couple of answers wrong. You can't stop beating yourself up for those two or three mistakes.
- You get an assignment back from your teachers, and they say you need to organize your ideas better. They have made numerous positive comments, but you get stuck on the bad ones.

Disqualifying the Positive: This is refusing to give positives the weight they merit.

Examples:

- Gerard said I was pretty. He was probably just being nice.
- Ana invited me to her party. She probably only invited me because Fatima is my friend.

Jumping to Conclusions: This is when you form conclusions without proper evidence.

Examples:

- Noor hardly spoke to me today. It's probably because her birthday is coming up, and she doesn't want to invite me to the party.
- Ms. Bailey was looking at my shoes today. I bet she thinks they're ugly and that I have no dress sense.

Magnification or Minimization: Exaggerating or minimizing the importance of things.

Examples:

- You win a coveted science prize at school but convince yourself that it's no big deal.
- You don't score a goal at today's soccer match, and you're convinced you've ruined your team's chance to make it to the finals.

Emotional Reasoning: This involves thinking that because you feel something, it has to be true.

Examples:

- I feel jealous that my friend Tania has made friends with the new girl at school, so I am sure she no longer likes me.
- I feel guilty, so I must have done something bad.

Should Statements: You make statements about things you (or others) "should" or "must" do.

Examples:

- I should get fitter.
- She should listen to me more.

Labeling and Mislabeling: You judge yourself or others because of isolated or infrequent instances or experiences.

Examples:

- You call yourself "stupid" for forgetting to pick someone up.
- You label a friend "selfish" because they had to do something for their parents, and they weren't able to listen to you one day.

Personalization: You take things personally or blame yourself without any logical reason to do so.

Examples:

- Your friends had a bad time at a concert, and you assume it's your fault.
- Your teacher asks everyone to read a poem to the class, and you assume she's set that task because she knows you don't like getting up in front of your class.

Control Fallacies: You can either believe you have no control over your own life and what happens or that you are in complete control/you are responsible for everything and everybody. Both fallacies can be damaging.

Examples:

- "There's no point in trying to get fit because I have no control over my body."
- "If I'm absent from school today, the group I'm working on the project with won't get anything done."

The Fairness Fallacy: You judge every experience by how fair you think it is, and you feel negative whenever you think something unfair has happened.

Examples:

- "The man at the counter served another client when I was here first. I'm fuming. That's unfair!"
- "The teacher chose Gem for the lead role in the musical when Jenny sings better."

Blaming: When things go wrong, it's always someone else's fault. You fail to understand that others do not have a greater power to affect your life than you do.

Examples:

- Saying to a friend, "You made me feel bad."
- Thinking: *She's the reason I got an anxiety attack today.*

The Change Fallacy: This is when you expect others will change to suit you.

Examples:

- If I keep asking Linda to do so, she will start being more thoughtful.
- I can stop Sunny from crying when he loses a wrestling match.

Always Being Right: You believe you have to be right; otherwise, it is a slight against you.

Examples:

- You feel that your best friend isn't as supportive as you'd like her to be. Your sibling disagrees. You get angry at your sibling because she should acknowledge all the evidence you're giving her and agree with you.
- You think that Millie Bobby Brown is a great actor, but your friend can't stand her. You get deeply annoyed when she criticizes Millie's acting in *Stranger Things* and say, "You're ignorant. You don't know anything about acting."

When you're upset about something, check yourself frequently. Ask yourself if you could be engaging in cognitive distortion. Try to depersonalize the situation and imagine you were a third party viewing the situation. Do something relaxing or enjoyable and get back to the situation later. Try to see if you can do so without using negative filters.

Exercises to End Negative Thought Patterns

It's time to get back to CBT and other thought-based activities. In this chapter, we will focus on exercises and worksheets that encourage you to think about things more positively.

Exercise One: Daily Mood Check

Check your mood various times a day. Always check at the same time. To make it easier, you might do so when you wake up, when you're on your way to school, at break time, after school, and when you're about to go to bed. When you notice a negative thought, ask yourself questions like:[21]

---

[21] Silber, 2021.

- Why am I thinking this/What is its purpose?
- How can I make this thought more positive?

Example:

More Positive Thoughts

Trigger	Automatic thought	The purpose of this thought	How can I make this thought more positive?
My teacher said I didn't do as well on the exam as I could have.	I'm hopeless and slow. I'll never catch up with the smart kids.	I may feel like I haven't studied as efficiently as I could have for exams.	I have performed well in this subject in the past. To catch up, all I need to do is spend half an hour a day going over the book. I am a capable student, always do well when I plan well for things, and stick to my study schedule.
Dad couldn't take me to school today, so I had to take the bus.	I hate getting the bus to school.	There is no deeper purpose to this thought; I am simply tired, and the bus takes a long time to get to school.	"I might use this bus ride to do a five-minute breathing section with my Breathe app."

Your turn, for this exercise, think about three recent events where you got: 1) Angry, 2) Sad, 3) Afraid. What triggered these emotions? Write down the events and proceed with answering the prompt questions in the table as shown on my example.

Trigger	Automatic thought	The purpose of this thought	How can I make this thought more positive?

Exercise Two: Watch Your Thoughts

When intrusive thoughts take over your calm, practice this mindful exercise.[22] Notice your breath or (if you're walking) your footsteps for around ten seconds. Notice the things around you—open your senses to the sights, sounds, and textures that surround you. Now turn your attention back to your breath or footsteps.

Exercise Three: The Five-Minute Cognitive Distortion Destroyer

Nip cognitive distortions in the bud before they ruin your day by filling in these three columns. This exercise only takes five minutes! Below is the table and an example.[23]

The 5-Min. Cognitive Distortion Destroyer

Negative Self-Talk/Negative Thought	I'm new at school and nobody likes me. I sat with Jim and his group, and they hardly said a word to me. I'll never fit in. They're a bunch of arrogant, rude idiots. It's so unfair that they never make me feel included when I've done nothing wrong to them.
Cognitive Filters	• The Fairness Fallacy • Overgeneralization • Jumping to conclusions • Labeling
Rational Response	My day could have gone better, but maybe Jim and his friends take a bit longer to get to know people. Tomorrow, I might try to sit with Will, who seemed very friendly on my first day of school. I won't discount Jim's group, but I will try to get to know everyone little by little.

---

[22] Cleveland Clinic, 2019.
[23] Aswell, 2020.

Here is an example scenario you can work on: You are with your friends and someone said something hurtful towards you. She/He did not intentionally hurt you but it hurt anyway. Has this happened to you? Think back to the memory and recognize what negative thought you had.

Exercise Four: Eight Questions: Challenging Negative Thoughts

Negative thoughts affect your mood, and they can also be triggers for anxiety and depression. When you find yourself saying negative things to yourself, ask yourself eight questions, writing your answer down in your journal.[24]

1. Is there objective evidence for my thought?

2. Is there any objective evidence that counters my thought?

3. Is my thought likely, or am I exaggerating what is actually true?

4. Am I making a conclusion when some evidence may be missing?

5. Did someone pass this thought or belief to me? Are they a trustworthy source?

6. What would a friend think about this situation? Would they see it differently?

7. If I view this situation more positively, how does it change?

8. How important will this be two weeks from now, two months from now, and two years from now?

---

[24] Therapist Aid, n.d.

Exercise Five: Five Questions: The Worry Worksheet

When you are worried about something, you can assume that the very worst outcome will occur. In fact, your worst fear may never come to fruition. When you are worried about something, ask yourself six questions, writing your answer down in your journal.[25]

1. What are you worried about?

2. What are signs that your worst fear won't come true?

3. If the very worst thing doesn't happen, what will probably occur instead?

4. If the very worst thing happens, how will you deal with it? Will you be alright anyway?

5. Now that you have completed the exercise, do you feel less worried?

Exercise Six: Take Your Thought to Court

If you want to be a lawyer or you are interested in court cases, why not bring your thought to court? In this fun exercise, you will act as a defense attorney, a prosecuting attorney, and a judge. The aim is to nullify negative thoughts and biases, so you can reap the benefits of positive thinking.[26]

---

[25] Therapist Aid, n.d.
[26] Therapist Aid, n.d.

Take Your Thought to Court

The aim is to nullify negative thoughts and biases so you can reap the benefits of positive thinking.

What is your thought?

_____

_____

_____

How would you defend this thought if you were a defense attorney? Use evidence in your arguments!	How would you attack the validity of this thought if you were a prosecuting attorney? Use evidence in your arguments!

The judge's verdict

_____

_____

_____

Exercise Seven: Managing Your Emotions by Checking the Facts

This exercise encourages you to focus on your emotions and the role that false assumptions can play in shaping them. Fill in the following table to manage your emotions.[27]

Managing Your Emotions by Checking the Facts

The event that triggered my emotion	My sister told her friend Simone that I had had a big fight with my best friend, Sandra. She knows I don't like her talking about my personal matters to her friends.
How I interpreted the event.	I thought that my sister had betrayed me. I was furious and resolved never to tell her anything again. I thought that my sister was out to get me and humiliate me in front of others. I threatened my sister to tell everyone some of her secrets.
Does my emotion and its intensity match the facts surrounding the situation, or does it just match by assumptions about the situation?	Perhaps I reacted too intensely to what my sister did. She explained that she wasn't gossiping. Her friend suggested inviting Sandra to our pajama party, and my sister unwittingly told her we were not getting along. I just assumed she had bad intentions when she didn't. Next time, I will express my disappointment without raising my voice or threatening my sister.

---

[27] Therapist Aid, n.d.

YOUR TURN!

The event that triggered my emotion	
How I interpreted the event.	
Does my emotion and its intensity match the facts surrounding the situation, or does it just match my assumptions about the situation?	

Exercise Eight: Healthy Emotional Expression

The aim of this exercise is to encourage you to express your emotions in a healthy way.[28] Think of an event that triggered a strong emotion. Write down an example of a healthy and an unhealthy way to express your emotions. Write the consequences of both ways of expressing emotions.

Healthy Emotional Expression

Triggering Event	Emotion
My close friend criticizes me to our classmates, and they tell me about it. Specifically, she tells them that I talk too much in class.	I get furious, disappointed, and distraught.

---

[28] Therapist Aid, n.d.

Healthy expression of the emotion	Results
Talking to my friend and saying I felt let down that she had spoken to others about me.	My friend acknowledges it was wrong and explains she criticized me because she was angry at me for not calling her the day before like I said I would. I apologize for that, she apologizes for talking to others, and we agree to talk directly to each other the next time we feel let down.

Unhealthy expression of the emotion	Results
I criticize my friend right back to our classmates. Next, I take my friend and call her a disloyal and bad friend.	We don't speak to each other for various weeks and continue to trash each other to others. The friendship is broken as there is no longer any trust.

YOUR TURN!

Triggering Event	Emotion

Healthy Expression of the Emotion	Results

Unhealthy Expression of the Emotion	Results

Exercise Nine: Solving Problems

It is easy to lose your calm when a problem comes along, and you are confused as to exactly what the issue is and how you can solve it. Rather than rushing to identify a solution, follow the seven-step method to find a solution that is truly useful for yourself, and other people involved. Use this sheet to define the problem, check the facts surrounding it, figure out your desired outcome, think of solutions, choose the one you think is best, put your chosen solution into action, and evaluate the results of your solution.[29]

Solving problems

Describe the problematic situation.	My classmates and I have been given a group project at school. The teacher has randomly assigned students to groups of four. Two of the students in my group refuse to do any work.
Check the facts to make sure you know what the problem really is.	The facts are that you and your friend Tristan have done all the research for your project. The others have not started yet and it's been a full week.
Identify your goal or desired outcome.	Your goal is for everyone to do their share and to prepare an excellent project.

---

[29] Eden Counseling, n.d.

Brainstorm three to five solutions to the problem.	Together with Tristan, you come up with the following options: • You will request to form your own group and inform the teacher that the other students aren't collaborating. • You'll finish the job and write their names on it. • You'll complete the assignment but leave their names out so the teacher will know they made no contribution. • You will hold a meeting and write down the exact tasks that need to be completed. You will each decide to take on an equal number of tasks and meet in two days to check your progress.
Choose one solution.	You pick the last solution-to make sure everyone knows exactly what they have to do so that there is no confusion and roles are clear.
Test the solution.	The project is a success. You discover that the students who didn't initially want to work are talented in other areas. For instance, one student might be a good graphic designer, and they might enjoy designing the project once the other persons in the group have completed their research. Take note: If the plan does not work and the students still refuse to pull their weight, then solution one—telling the teacher and asking to regroup—may be more beneficial.
Record if the solution worked for you. If not, try another solution in your list.	Your team agrees to complete the assigned tasks, and you meet frequently to check each other's progress. The students who previously refused to do work have done some work, and you give them helpful suggestions for the parts they haven't done. You share useful links and/or use Google Meets to keep working after class ends.

YOUR TURN!

Describe the problematic situation.	
Check the facts to make sure you know what the problem really is.	
Identify your goal or desired outcome.	
Brainstorm three to five solutions to the problem.	
Choose one solution.	
Test the solution.	
Record if the solution worked for you. If not, try another solution in your list.	

Exercise Ten: Two-Step Negative Thought Buster

This exercise is a quick, two-step activity that challenges you to replace negative thoughts with a rational counterstatement.[30]

Two-Step Negative Thought Buster

Negative Thought	Rational Counterstatement
I'll never make friends. Everyone else seems more interesting than me.	I don't know anyone at this summer camp, but everyone else is in the same boat as me. At school, it took me a couple of weeks to get to know people, but I made a great group of friends and I will do the same at this camp.
I didn't play volleyball well today. They will probably kick me out of the team.	All my team members have bad days. I was tired because it was exam week. As soon as I feel more rested, I will play with my usual zest and energy.

YOUR TURN!

Negative Thought	Rational Counterstatement

---

[30] Therapist Aid, n.d.

Returning to Tim

If you go back to Tim's story, you will probably be able to identify a few cognitive distortions he uses in his thinking. For instance, he tends to focus on the bad things that happen in his life and discount the good things.

You may think (and you'd be right) that Tim has many valid reasons for feeling unworthy. He has had little praise and too much pressure placed on him. Tim has work to do, since he needs to understand how his childhood experiences have influenced him to adopt harmful thought and belief patterns. By reframing these thoughts and beliefs and committing to eliminate harmful filters, he can start working on being kind and compassionate to himself, and to understand that nobody deserves to be belittled or to be forced to live up to someone else's expectations.

You now have a good idea of how the way you think can affect your emotions or actions. In Chapter Three, we will analyze the important role that your beliefs can play in your success, happiness, and well-being.

Chapter Three

Challenging Negative Beliefs

"It's so important to identify beliefs.
Because once you identify [a negative belief], once you bring it into the light, you will see it doesn't belong to you:
- *That it came from your parents;*
- *It came from your family;*
- *It came from your society;*
- *It came from your friends;*
- *And you bought into it. But it isn't yours.*
Holding on to something that isn't yours is called theft. Don't be a belief thief!" – **Bashar**

The successful motivator and speaker Tony Robbins once said, "The only thing that's keeping you from getting what you want is the story you keep telling yourself ."[31] I have included two quotes in starting this chapter because they encapsulate two important points about negative self-beliefs:

1. They arise from childhood patterns and past experiences.
2. You are responsible for keeping them alive.

---

[31] Finerman, 2019.

Lara's Story

Lara is a woman in her 20s who grew up feeling like she was never good enough. She was raised by her narcissistic mom Linda, who demanded admiration from others and believed she was above them.

She exploited her children, using their achievements to bolster her own ego. She often put Lara down and did not respect her boundaries. She also competed with her, and it only got worse when Lara hit her teens and started blossoming into a young woman.

At school, Lara achieved good grades and had a small but solid group of friends. She got into college on a scholarship, yet after graduating, her career seemed to be going nowhere. She lacked the confidence she needed to apply to good jobs, seemed to be attracted to partners who didn't respect her, and didn't know what to do with her life.

There were good companies she could have applied for, but she felt she just wasn't a winner and wouldn't be able to compete with more confident candidates. She was scared that during the recruitment process, those hiring recruits would see how useless, insecure, and dumb she actually was.

Not so fun fact

The National Science Foundation reports that our brains can produce as many as 50,000 thoughts per day. Around ninety-five percent of these thoughts are repeated daily.

You have the power to decide how you think and what is possible or impossible. Your thoughts transform into beliefs, and the set of beliefs you live by forms your mindset and influences your behaviors. This is how reality is created.[32]

What Is a Limiting Belief?

A limiting belief is a thought that you think is the absolute truth, and it stops you from doing specific things. A limiting belief does not have to be about yourself. It could be about your colleagues, friends, family members, or partner.[33]

Common Negative Core Beliefs

Core beliefs are the deeply held beliefs that affect how we interpret situations. If you have positive core beliefs, you tend to have positive thoughts and behaviors. The same applies to negative core beliefs; they influence how you think and behave.

Typical negative core beliefs include:

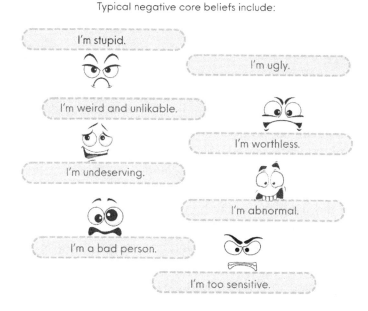

I'm stupid.

I'm ugly.

I'm weird and unlikable.

I'm worthless.

I'm undeserving.

I'm abnormal.

I'm a bad person.

I'm too sensitive.

---

[32] Finerman, 2019.
[33] Wooll, 2022.

Your beliefs, thoughts, emotions, and behaviors work in
this order:

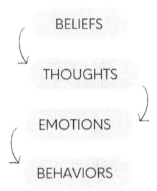

BELIEFS

THOUGHTS

EMOTIONS

BEHAVIORS

What Causes Limiting Beliefs?

There are many reasons why limiting beliefs may arise. Common
causes include:

Family Values and Beliefs

We all learn values and beliefs from our family, often through the
example of our parents. Sometimes, our parents don't intend to instill
these beliefs in us purposefully. For instance, your parents might
prioritize getting into a good college and making a good living when you
are older. A grandparent may repeatedly warn you against trusting
others (and tell you stories of how trusting the wrong person got them
burned in the past). You may be close to an uncle who values giving
back to the community and takes you along to fundraising events, beach
clean-ups, and other means of being generous with those around you.
Your older sister may be into heavy metal and alternative music, and
she may take you to concerts and play all her favorite songs at home.
The values of all these people may shape your own beliefs and shape
the goals you aim for in life.

Your Experiences

How you experience certain situations has a big impact on how you view them in the future. For instance, you may have a big library at home full of great books from all genres and a wide array of authors. Your parents may be avid readers, and you may have afternoons where you gather in the library with a snack and drink, with everyone reading their favorite book. Another teen, however, may live in a home where there are few books, which are all boring or difficult to read. Their parents may insist that they read, and the result may be that when they are older, they hate books and remember the feeling of being forced into reading.

Alternatively, you may have a parent who's a self-confessed foodie. They may bring you out to eat at a new place every weekend until your palate becomes quite sophisticated, and you know how to distinguish between different quality foods and cuisines styles. When you are older, you may enjoy saving up to splurge at a Michelin-star restaurant with your partner. For you, dining out may be synonymous with good times and family bonding. A teen whose parent never valued sophisticated cuisine, however, may see dining at expensive places as "a waste of money." It is easy to see how there is no right or wrong; it all depends on the lens you are looking through. Sometimes, it makes little difference if you are using one filter or another. However, in some areas of life, using a negative filter can make a big difference in your ability to achieve goals or simply feel confident and happy.

Your Education

If you have great teachers, you may view learning as fun, enriching, and captivating. Imagine, however, that your teacher doesn't like their job, enters the classroom with little zest, and spends most of their time asking you to read the textbook yourself and just answer the questions. It is easy to see how you may give this teacher's values and beliefs little importance. On the other hand, imagine that you have a teacher that's fun, inspiring, and humorous. They enter the classroom with new activities, have an open mind, and are as interested in what you have to say as they are in sharing information. It is easy to see how a teacher like this would have a far greater impact on your own thoughts, beliefs, and values.

Examples of Limiting Beliefs

Below are five examples of what limiting beliefs look and sound like when held by teens in different situations.

1. **A Teen Job-Seeker:** "I would love to work at that coffee shop over the summer, but I know they won't hire me. I am sure they won't hire someone who doesn't have experience. Moreover, I can only work on weekends, and they may want someone who is available all the time. I walked in and left my CV at another café last year, and they never called me. What will be different this time?"

2. **A Student:** "I would love to do an advanced math course, but I'm too slow to succeed in that class. Everyone else there is so much smarter than me."

3. **A Potential Senior-Class President:** "I would love to run for school president, but I'm not popular enough to win. I have so many good ideas I would like to present, but I'm too shy to communicate my ideas well. Moreover, Tommy is running for president, and he always wins everything. I am too embarrassed to run—what if I only get a handful of votes?"

4. **A Footballer:** "I would like to be on the football team, but try-outs are next week, and I don't think I'm fit enough. I had a look the other day at some of the guys who were playing, and they are ripped. I have been training hard, but I am sure that when I get there, I won't be as fit as the rest of the guys."

5. **A Student:** "The teacher handed back our exams, and I saw that she had marked some questions that were right as wrong. I would like to run through the questions with her, but I am sure that if I do so, she will see me as argumentative and take it out on me in the long run by giving me a lower grade than I deserve."

What is common in all these situations? A host of self-limiting beliefs are being taken as fact. Can you imagine what would happen if each of these teens challenged their beliefs and forged ahead with their dreams?

How Can We Recognize a Limiting Belief?

In order to recognize a limiting belief, you need to know what it looks, sounds, and feels like and stop it from interfering with your wants and needs. Stop negative beliefs in their tracks by:

1. **Being Aware of the Words You Say:** Do they serve a purpose? Are they moving you towards your goal or against it? Are they encouraging you to do nothing and keep things exactly as they are? If so, it is a good sign that they are limiting beliefs.

2. **Being Honest:** Is the story you are telling yourself fully true? Are you making sweeping statements without testing if they are authentic or not?

3. **Sticking to the Facts:** For instance, in example 3, you say you are sure your classmates won't vote for you, but have you actually presented your ideas to them? Have you talked to them about the changes they wish to effect and planned a strategy of how to make it happen? Or does all this take so much work that you are fooling yourself into taking the easy way out?

4. **Taking a Pause**: Do you say three or four negative things to yourself before you even realize what you are saying? Be clued up to negative thoughts and beliefs. They can roll off your tongue

or fill your head in seconds. Take a pause and say, "Okay, I realize I'm saying negative things to myself right now." Understand that the words you say can affect everything from what you do next to the long-term decisions you make. Ultimately, the goal is to reframe the negative beliefs into positive ones, so you can achieve all your goals—small and large ones.

The Three Types of Negative Beliefs

As I wrote above, beliefs don't have to be about yourself and what you can or can't achieve. Below are three types of negative beliefs:[34]

Beliefs About Yourself

Examples: "I'm too slow, not smart enough, not good-looking enough, not charming enough."

Who might have this type of belief? Someone who has been heavily criticized or abused. Someone who has grown up with a narcissistic or manipulative adult.

Beliefs About Others

Examples: "She's bitter, untrustworthy, envious."

Who might have this type of belief? Someone who has been through a traumatic event or who has been hurt deeply by one or more people.

---

[34] Branch & Wilson, 2021.

Beliefs About the World

Examples: "The world is a terrible place. It is full of bad things, and there are dangers everywhere."

Who might have this type of belief? Someone who has lived through trauma or survived in threatening environments.

These core beliefs can intersect. For instance, you may feel that a friend you trusted is now envious of you. Your belief in the essential badness of the world and human beings compounds this belief.

Exercises to Challenge Negative Beliefs

It's now time to stop negative beliefs in their track by working on yourself. These exercises and activities will help you see life through a more balanced lens.

Exercise One: Following the Downward Arrow: Finding Your Negative Core Belief

This exercise encourages you to discover the hidden meaning behind negative thoughts and painful experiences or situations.[35]

1. Define a negative automatic thought or outcome that is bothering you. *Example: I will never have a group of close friends.*
2. Ask what it says about you. *When I try to get to know people, they reject me.*
3. Ask yourself what the answer to #2 says about you. *They reject me because there is something about me that puts them off.*
4. Ask what the answer to #3 says about you. *I'm a failure.* **THIS IS YOUR CORE BELIEF!**

---

[35] Branch & Wilson, 2021.

Sometimes, you will find the meaning of a negative belief in one or two questions. The aim of this exercise is to get used to questioning the way in which you may allow painful situations and thoughts to make valuable judgments against you. After finding your negative core belief, it will be easier for you to counteract it using arguments to nullify or challenge it.

Exercise Two: Reflecting on Negative Life Experiences

Negative beliefs are the broad judgments you make about yourself, many of which are based on negative experiences you may have had in your early years.[36] You can find out more about how you view yourself by understanding how specific experiences gave rise to your negative core beliefs.

Take your journal and fill in the following information:

1. What negative experience negatively impacted my self-esteem? *Example: The divorce of my parents.*

2. Did this experience lead me to see that something was wrong with me? If so, what negative things did they lead me to think or believe? *It led me to believe that I was difficult or troublesome, and that caused my parents to argue and get a divorce.*

3. Can I remember specific situations from the past that accompany the negative feelings I have about myself? What do my memories of these situations say about me as a person? *When I feel the worst about myself, I remember my parents arguing, and I recall that some of the arguments were about me. These memories tell me that I was a cause of anguish for them.*

---

[36] Lim et al., 2005.

4. Is there a specific person that I associate with how I feel about myself? Did that person say specific words that shaped my beliefs? What does the way they treat me say about me as a person? *I remember when my friend told me I was so overweight he did not want me to be in a photograph he was taking. This treatment suggested I was worthless.*

Exercise Three: Reflecting on My Negative Core Beliefs

In the heading earlier in this chapter called Examining Negative Beliefs, I gave various examples of core beliefs that stopped teens from achieving their goals. Take the boy who wanted to run for class president but was so afraid of rejection he never presented his candidature. For Exercise 3, I want you to take one negative core belief about yourself, then ask yourself the following questions:[37]

1. What would happen if my negative expectations were to come true? What would this say about me as a human being? *Example: If nobody voted for me for class president, I would feel like a loser. It would mean I was useless and unlikable.*

2. If I didn't avoid going for my goals, what would I be revealing that could make me feel uncomfortable? *If I ran for President, I would risk showing others that their opinions matter to me. I am scared to reveal that I want to be a leader and make positive changes in the school.*

3. What would I tell a friend if they answered the way I did in question #1? *Only one person wins this type of competition, but it doesn't mean that those who don't win aren't liked or appreciated by others.*

---

[37] Schaffner, 2020.

4. What would I tell a friend if they wanted to go for a goal but were scared of showing their vulnerabilities? *I would tell them that you can't really progress in life unless you take some risks. By running for president, they could meet new people, practice their public speaking skills, and enjoy asking a friend to do a cool dance to back their campaign.*

Fun Film Suggestion: Have you seen *Napoleon Dynamite* yet? The film is all about a friend who helps his BFF run for class President by doing the funniest dance in history!

Exercise Four: What is Stopping Me from Being Kind to Myself?

Self-kindness has a myriad of benefits. Studies have shown, for instance, that it is a powerful antidote to perfectionism.[38]

Take your journal and write your answers to the following questions:

1. What is stopping me from being as kind to myself as I am to the people I love? *Example: I don't feel worthy of self-love.*

2. What do I tell myself when I try to be kinder to myself? *I tell myself that my childhood experiences (receiving lots of criticism) make me question my self-worth but that I am a good person who deserves love like everyone else.*

3. What do my reactions to exercising self-kindness say about how I view myself? *Working on my self-worth will help me feel more worthy of love and up the chances that I will receive it.*

---
[38] Ferrari et al., 2018.

Exercise Five: Busting Unhelpful Rules

Setting rules and sticking to them is helpful in many ways. For instance, you may set rules about how long you use screens, how many hours you need to study for an exam, or what time you should exercise. These rules all help you achieve your goals. They are realistic, positive, and achievable.

Rules can be unhelpful, though, whenever they are too strict or difficult to follow. For instance, holding the belief, "I can never get anything less than an A+ on tests," is damaging because sometimes, even though you study hard and prepare well, you may get a couple of questions wrong. This rigid rule will only result in disappointment and self-blame because it is unreasonable.[39]

In the exercise below, I want you to identify unhelpful rules and understand how they can affect your happiness and well-being.

1. Write down the unhelpful rules or assumptions that you would benefit from changing or adapting.
    Example: *If I don't get straight As, it means I'm not smart.*
2. Where did this rule or assumption come from?
    Example: My parents expressed disappointment if I brought home a less-than-perfect report card.
3. How is this negative assumption harming me?
    Example: I sometimes avoid going for my goal because I am afraid, I will fail.
4. If I broke this rule, what would that mean about me as a human being?
    Example: If I got a B instead of an A, it would simply mean that I am human. Nobody is perfect all the time.
5. How can I make this rule more flexible?

---

[39] Fursland et al., 2009.

Examples: Not getting straight As does not mean I'm not smart.

Trying my best is okay—I will achieve better results in some areas of my life than others.

My focus is on eating healthily and staying active, not on strict calorie counting or losing an unreasonable amount of weight in a short amount of time.

Exercise Six: Adjusting Negative Core Beliefs

This exercise aims to highlight how you can change negative core beliefs into positive ones.[40]

1. Write down one negative core belief. Beneath this belief, write down how strongly you feel it at the moment, what situations tend to provoke it, and how it makes you feel. Next, list three pieces of evidence that are contrary to your negative core belief.

   For example: I'm unlovable. I feel this intensely at the moment because I wasn't invited to a party my other friends are attending today. It makes me feel like the odd girl out. I tend to feel unlovable when people do not include me in social gatherings.

Three pieces of evidence that I'm not unlovable:

- My close friends say I am trustworthy and a great friend.
- My little sister adores me and always wants to hang around me.
- My aunt says she has a soft spot for me.

2. Write down a balanced core belief that is positive and realistic and that more accurately reflects you.

---

[40] Schaffner, 2020.

For example: I like to reflect on study material and do my own research, then come to conclusions. I have a reflective learning style. I am learning to respect others' boundaries and set my own.

I am better at some sports than others, but I can enjoy playing all sports with others.

Exercise Seven: Finding Evidence for Positive Core Beliefs

This exercise will focus on looking at the "evidence" we use to form negative beliefs and push us to consider other evidence that can help us understand a situation from a broader perspective. Think of one negative belief (for instance, "I'm not a good friend" or "I'm not smart enough") and fill in the following table: Fill in the right column.[41]

Why do I have this belief?	New ways of understanding the "evidence" for this belief
Are current problems or mental conditions like anxiety or stress the basis of my belief?	Could I be experiencing these problems for reasons other than my personal flaws? For example: I could not be a poor friend right now, but rather more irritated or distant with people since I recently lost a dear family member and am feeling miserable.
Am I being hard on myself because I am struggling to get through a problem by myself?	Is there anything wrong with seeking help when you need it? Do I judge others when they ask for help? For example: Seeking support from others is a good thing. When my friends have issues, I am always happy to lend a helping hand.
Am I being so hard on myself because of past mistakes (for instance, because I got poor grades last term, procrastinated for exams, or told a friend's secret to someone else)?	Is it reasonable to be so hard on myself for making mistakes? For example: I can use my mistakes to formulate a better study strategy, or I can use the experience with my friend to prioritize discretion when a friend shares private information with me.

---

[41] Schaffner, 2020.

Positive Core Beliefs Cont...

Am I mad at myself for a skill I don't have (for instance, finding it hard to follow a choreography, not being able to sing on key, and similar)?	Is it reasonable to base my self-esteem on areas I perceive myself as weak in? For example: Just because I'm not good at singing does not make me bad at everything. Everyone has their strengths and weaknesses.
Am I mad at myself because of my physical appearance or personality (for instance, my body type, the fact that I am an introvert, or the fact that I am sensitive)?	Is it reasonable to base my self-esteem on my physical appearance or personality? I don't judge others for being who they are, so why should I judge myself?
Am I mad or disappointed with myself because I compare myself to other people?	Is it fair to base my self-esteem on whether or not I am better than someone else at something? For example: Just because my friend is confident does not mean they are better than me. We all have areas of our personality that we can improve through practice and experience.
Does the way others treat me affect the way I see myself?	What are other reasons (other than my personal flaws) that people treat me that way? For example: The way people treat me says more about the type of person they are than who I am.
Does the behavior of others (for instance, my parents) affect how I view myself?	Is it fair to judge myself because of others' actions? For example: As much as I try to help, I am not responsible for their behavior.
Have I experienced a big loss that affected my self-worth (for instance, the break-up of a friendship)?	Is it fair to base my self-worth on one painful experience? For example: Marla decided she no longer wanted to be friends with me, but I have other friends and family members who love me unconditionally.

YOUR TURN!

Why do I have this belief?	New ways of understanding the "evidence" for this belief
Are current problems or mental conditions like anxiety or stress the basis of my belief?	
Am I being hard on myself because I am struggling to get through a problem by myself?	
Am I being so hard on myself because of past mistakes (for instance, because I got poor grades last term, procrastinated for exams, or told a friend's secret to someone else)?	
Am I mad at myself for a skill I don't have (for instance, finding it hard to follow a choreography, not being able to sing on key, and similar)?	
Am I mad at myself because of my physical appearance or personality (for instance, my body type, the fact that I am an introvert, or the fact that I am sensitive)?	

Continue Activity here...

Am I mad or disappointed with myself because I compare myself to other people?	
Does the way others treat me affect the way I see myself?	
Does the behavior of others (for instance, my parents) affect how I view myself?	
Have I experienced a big loss that affected my self-worth (for instance, the break-up of a friendship)?	

Exercise Eight: Disputing Irrational Beliefs

Rational beliefs are based on facts, and they help us achieve our short- and long-term goals and feel the emotions we want to feel. Remember that it is **the way you interpret an event** that causes your emotional reaction. As stated by the ancient scholar Epictetus, "Men are disturbed not by things, but by the views which they take of them."[42]

---

[42] Schaffner, 2020.

To dispute an irrational belief:

1. Define an irrational belief that pops up frequently in your mind.

2. Ask yourself—is it rational to support this belief? Who supports this idea, and what authority do they have to do so?

3. Is there any evidence that this belief is false?

4. What is the worst thing that could happen if I don't get what I want?

5. What positive things could I make happen if I don't get what I want?

Exercise Nine: Filling in a Table of Core Beliefs

Sometimes, it can be hard to identify the core beliefs that are hurting you. Below are three columns with beliefs about yourself, your surroundings, and other people. Tick the negative beliefs that ring a bell and think about how you can dispute them.[43]

Core Beliefs About Yourself	Core Beliefs About the World Around You	Core Beliefs About Others
I will never satisfy my parents.	Nobody cares about my opinions.	My friends/family need me to protect them.
I need to hide how I feel.	I can't trust my teachers.	My friends should protect me and defend me.
I find it hard to love others.	I need to control my environment, or I find it hard to control my feelings.	I can't get on with someone whose interests are different from mine.
I am slow.	The world outside is dangerous.	Trusting others is unsafe.

---

[43] Positive Pyschology, n.d.

YOUR TURN!

Core Beliefs About Yourself	Core Beliefs About the World Around You	Core Beliefs About Others

Exercise Ten: What Are Your Most and Least Advantageous Beliefs?

List the three most advantageous and least advantageous beliefs you hold. Say why they are a help or a hindrance.

Returning to Lara

Lara's problems were deep-seated, so she chose to see a therapist. She learned that many of her core beliefs were related to the unrealistic expectations her mom had set for her. Lara worked hard to reframe these beliefs into positive ones and worked up the courage to apply to many companies and learn how to "sell" herself at interviews. She was taken up by one of the city's top law firms, who were intrigued by the fact she was a certified scuba diver!

Now that you know how to counter negative thoughts and beliefs, it's time to experiment with healthy behaviors. Discover how to do so in Chapter 4!

Chapter Four

Changing Negative Behaviors

"Behavioral experimentation is widely regarded as the single most powerful way of changing cognitions." – Glenn Waller

BT encourages you to try out new thoughts and behaviors. For some people, thinking about things is the most effective way to manage emotions and behaviors. You may be different, but for most people, "doing" instead of "thinking" may be the best way forward. You may enjoy experimenting with new behavioral strategies and seeing how they affect your thoughts and emotions.

In reality, with CBT, you don't have to choose. You can try out a few exercises from Chapter 2 one day, for instance, and try the behavioral exercises provided in this chapter another day. As I mentioned in the introduction, I have provided a myriad of exercises in the book, and you can pick those which are most effective or enjoyable for you. But first, let's get to a story that epitomizes why Einstein was right when he said, "The definition of insanity is doing the same thing over and over again, but expecting different results."

My daughter, Claire, had always loved writing stories and poems, but she was always shy to share her work with anyone other than us (her family) or her best friends. Recently, however, a famed writer gave a writing workshop for students at Claire's college and (after running the decision over in her head various times) she opted to sign up.

She told me that she would stay up late at night worrying about the course and how she would perform, but she decided to take the plunge anyway, as she realized this was a once-in-a-lifetime opportunity. She knew that she would have to read her work to the class (and the writer) and that placed major pressure on her. However, she realized that writing stories and reading them to the same three people wasn't very stimulating, either.

What Scientists Say About Behavioral Change

Many scientists believe that behavioral changes are more powerful than those that are based on thought; through my experiences, I tend to agree with this observation. The academics P. Chadwick and colleagues have written, for instance,[44] "Beliefs rarely change as a result of intellectual challenge, but only through engaging emotions and behaving in new ways that produce evidence that confirm new beliefs." In other words, when you engage in new behaviors, you can find direct proof that something negative you thought or felt is false—in a very real, practical way.

---

[44] Chadwick et al., 1996.

What Negative Behaviors Do Teens Sometimes Display?

It is counter-productive to generalize about any age group. However, as I mentioned in the introduction, teens today are subject to various sources of stress. For instance, they spend many hours a day on screens.

Studies have shown, however, that constant exposure to devices like smartphones, PCs, and televisions can severely affect mental health and increase stress and anxiety (and sleep problems) in users of all ages. Excessive screen time is also linked to obesity, cardiovascular issues, poor stress regulation, and many more problems. Additional stressors for teens include parental stress to succeed at school, the wish to get into a good college, peer pressure at school, the wish to have more friends, climate change, and the recent pandemic. There are so many reasons that can push you to negative behaviors, such as:

- seeking solitude
- lashing out in anger
- being irritable
- raising your voice
- keeping issues inside until you explode and lash out at someone
- slamming doors
- and more

Feeling Angry Is Okay

Earlier, we spoke of the important role that anger can play in prompting us to make a change. Clinical Psychologist, Lauren Allerhand, states, "Anger is an important part of our emotional lives. But anger gets a bad rap because the urges that come with it — yelling, fighting, being unkind to others — can be destructive and upsetting."[45]

In addition to stress, anger is another normal part of adolescence, and it can be a healthy emotional response to outside stressors. As Psychologist and best-selling author Dr. Harriet Lerner said in her book Dance of Anger, "Anger is a signal, and it's one worth listening to."[46] The emotion of anger isn't bad per se, but it is often portrayed in a negative light because the behaviors that can result from it—including raising one's voice, fighting, and being unkind to others—can be hurtful to oneself and others.

When you feel angry:

- Don't try to suppress the feeling.
- Know that it doesn't mean there is something wrong with you.
- You can find safe, beneficial ways to use your anger to create a better life.

In Chapter 7, we will immerse ourselves in handy anger management exercises, but for now, it's important to be aware that anger is just another human emotion and that there is nothing wrong with feeling it.

Challenges for Teens Wishing to Regulate Their Emotions

In Chapter 1, I mentioned that factors such as brain maturation, hormonal surges, and inexperience when it comes to curbing the fight or flight response can all make emotional regulation more challenging during the teen years. Your home environment is also influential. For instance, if you grew up in a household in which people raised their voices to make a point, did not resolve conflicts positively, or did not respect others' limits, these patterns can become ingrained. They can

[45] Jacobson, n.d.
[46] Anger Alternatives, n.d.

be harder to shed as you grow older, but if you are aware of them and you decide to break free of them, you can progress in leaps and bounds.

What Do Effective Self-Regulators Do?

People who "self-regulate" are those that manage their emotions—positive and negative—in a confident, effective way. They tend to:[47]

- Behave in accordance with their values. For instance, if you value getting good grades, then you study hard, pay attention in class, and try to improve in areas you find more challenging.

- Know how to self-calm. When you manage your emotions well and a trigger arises (for instance, someone raises their voice at you, takes your things at school, or does not respect your refusal to do something), you know how to tell yourself, "Take it easy, don't lose your cool." You don't need somebody else to calm you down. When you feel stressed, you might take a break from the situation, try some controlled breathing, or go to a peaceful spot until you feel ready to tackle the issue again.

- Know how to lift their own spirits when they feel down. Feelings like sadness and disappointment are inevitable. However, it is important to know how to limit their effect on our well-being. For instance, when you feel sad, you might go for a run, watch your favorite influencer on YouTube, or call a friend. You can identify the things that lift your spirit, and you rely on these mood lifters when you're feeling down in the dumps.

- Maintain the door to communication open. You don't ghost people, become emotionally unavailable, or cut ties radically when tensions arise with others.

---

47 Cuncic, 2022.

- Persist through difficult times. You are aware that it is part of the human condition to have better and worse times in life, and you know that you will make it through difficult patches, as dark as they may seem.

- Do their best. Even though you are undertaking a task (or taking part in an activity) that isn't your favorite, you still try to do your best.

- Remain flexible and adapt to situations when they need to. You are okay if a plan doesn't go exactly as expected. You know that people and circumstances can be variable at times.

- See the good side of others. You don't apply negative filters to people. You try to see more of the things you have in common with them than the things you disagree about.

- Show their intentions clearly. You communicate your wants and needs assertively while still being respectful and kind.

- Take control of situations when they have to. If you are working on a group project and things are disorganized, you gather people together and work out how to get back on track.

- See challenges as opportunities. You know that some of the most important life lessons are obtained after a difficult or challenging experience.

Behavioral Exercises for Self-Regulation

Behavioral experiments frequently involve some form of exposure to a feared stimulus, which typically makes the learning process emotionally challenging.[48]

---

[48] Psychology Tools, n.d.

Some authors have proposed that the particular effectiveness of behavioral experiments is due to the combination of:

- **Physiological Arousal**—When you are aroused, you may have physiological reactions such as a rise in your heart rate and blood pressure.

- **Inhibitory Learning**—This type of learning happens when we understand that bad things don't always happen when something we fear occurs.

Many exercises involve identifying a target thought or belief, conducting an experiment, discussing the outcome, and finally, figuring out what you have learned. Let's jump into a few behavior-based exercises!

Exercise One: The Three Options Activity

When a crisis situation arises, you have one of the following three options. You can:[49]

1. **Approach:** *Example: A school friend gets angry at you because you auditioned for the school musical and got the role she wanted. You approach her to talk about why she is upset.*

2. **Avoid:** *You know your friend is mad at you, so you avoid her. She tries to call you a couple of days after her outburst, but you don't get on the phone. You sit with other people at lunch, so you don't have to come across her.*

3. **Attack:** *You go straight to your friend and call her a jealous cow. You tell her she is a bad friend because everyone else is happy for you.*

---

[49] Cuncic, 2022.

Which approach do you find yourself taking more often? If you avoid or attack, the next time a crisis arises, try giving the other person space and then approaching. Write down how this worked for you.

Exercise Two: Testing a Thought With Strategic Behavior

Earlier in this book, we mentioned how the way you think and feel can affect the way you act and vice-versa. We mentioned that irrational thoughts could sometimes lead us to make decisions that do not make us feel good (or stand in the way of our goals) in the long run. In this exercise, we will put our thoughts to the test by taking part in behavioral experiments.[50]

1. Planning the Experiment

    a. What is the thought you would like to test? *Example: I want to test if the new girl at school really doesn't like me.*
    b. How can you test this thought? *I might go up and talk to her at break time.*
    c. Predict the outcome. *I think she might be rude and not answer me kindly.*

2. Analyzing the Outcome of the Experiment

    a. What happened when you carried out the experiment (in other words, when you went up and talked to her)? *Example: She was nice, and I could see that she was shy. She told me she was finding it hard to make new friends at school.*
    b. Do you have a new thought as a result of the experiment? *The new girl is funny and kind. I don't think she dislikes me at all, and I will try to make her transition easier by introducing her to my other friends.*

---

[50] Therapist Aid, n.d.

Exercise Three: Following a Weekly Behavioral Activation Schedule

In this exercise, you are encouraged to choose a few useful behaviors you can embrace every day to grow as a person or achieve one or more goals. Having a schedule can be handy, especially if you sometimes procrastinate or if you are feeling low or unmotivated. Commit to ticking each activity off your list and reward yourself at the end of the week if you have completed most of them.[51]

Weekly Behavioral Activation Schedule

○ DAY : Monday
ACTIVITY: Go for a run after school.

○ DAY : Tuesday
ACTIVITY: Call Tristan up for a chat. Practice my piano playing.

○ DAY : Wednesday
ACTIVITY: Ask a friend if he can come over on the weekend. Join the free outdoor yoga class with my mom at the park after class.

○ DAY : Thursday
ACTIVITY: Sign up for the debate club.

○ DAY : Friday
ACTIVITY: Ask a friend if she wants to come to the school musical with me on Saturday.

○ DAY : Saturday
ACTIVITY: Go scuba diving with my sister.

○ DAY : Sunday
ACTIVITY: Make a healthy lunch for my family.

---

[51] Therapist Aid, n.d.

YOUR TURN!

DAY : Monday
ACTIVITY:

DAY : Tuesday
ACTIVITY:

DAY : Wednesday
ACTIVITY:

DAY : Thursday
ACTIVITY:

DAY : Friday
ACTIVITY:

DAY : Saturday
ACTIVITY:

DAY : Sunday
ACTIVITY:

Exercise Four: One-A-Day Activity Sheet

If you like to be more spontaneous, this exercise might be more up your alley than Exercise Three. Its purpose is the same, but it gives you a host of ideas that can be helpful if you don't know what to put on your list. Just circle and complete one activity every day, every couple of days, or per week.

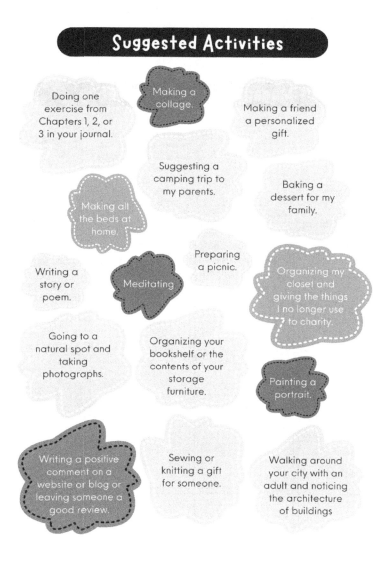

Suggested Activities

Doing one exercise from Chapters 1, 2, or 3 in your journal.

Making a collage.

Making a friend a personalized gift.

Suggesting a camping trip to my parents.

Baking a dessert for my family.

Making all the beds at home.

Writing a story or poem.

Meditating

Preparing a picnic.

Organizing my closet and giving the things I no longer use to charity.

Going to a natural spot and taking photographs.

Organizing your bookshelf or the contents of your storage furniture.

Painting a portrait.

Writing a positive comment on a website or blog or leaving someone a good review.

Sewing or knitting a gift for someone.

Walking around your city with an adult and noticing the architecture of buildings

Exercise Five: Managing Triggers Healthily

Stressful or difficult situations can sometimes be triggers for unhealthy behaviors such as smoking, drinking, or other harmful activities. In this exercise, you are encouraged to analyze the way in which triggers can lead you to take part in harmful behaviors. It also asks you to come up with a healthier behavior to try out the next time the trigger arises.[52]

Managing Triggers Healthily

Trigger	What I used to deal with it.	Why did I behave that way? What did I want to gain or avoid?	Next time I will...
I was not invited to a party I was keen to attend.	I got home and refused to play with my younger brother.	I wanted to be left alone because I was feeling so bad.	Next time I will talk to someone about how I feel and be kinder to my little sibling, letting them know I can play with them in a couple of hours, but not right now.

---

[52] Therapist Aid, n.d.

Exercise Six: My Relaxation Record

Taking part in calming activities during the day can help you deal with the stress that remains when your "fight or flight" response is invoked. Try to choose one relaxing activity for the morning and one for the afternoon. Rate the activities you try from 1 to 10, so you can see which works the best for you.[53]

My Relaxation Record

DAY	Morning relaxation activity	Rate it from 1-10	Afternoon/ evening relaxation activity	Rate it from 1-10
Monday	Alternate nose breathing	7	Had a bubble bath	9
Tuesday				
Wednesday				
Thursday				
Friday				
Saturday				
Sunday				

---

[53] Psychology Tools, n.d.

Create a Behavior Contract

Talk with your parents and agree on a reward for demonstrating specific behavior. Sign the contract with them.[54] The contract might look something like this:

I,_____, will do my best to do the following to improve my happiness and wellbeing:

If I do this,_____will reward me by _____.

Exercise Eight: Choosing a Goal Using the SMART Goal-Setting Method

When deciding to experiment with new behaviors, it is important to set realistic goals. There is no point in pursuing goals that are excessively

---

[54] Psychology Tools, n.d.

hard. Setting goals involves striking a balance between what you want to achieve and the resources and time you have.[55]

A SMART goal is one that is:

- specific
- measurable
- achievable
- relevant
- time-bound (This just means that you should ideally set a deadline—it does not have to be excessively strict or unchangeable—for the accomplishment of your goals.)

Fill in this worksheet:

1. Write down your goal. *For example: "I want to run a mile in 11 minutes."*

2. Be specific. *"My goal is very specific."*

3. Make sure you can measure if you have achieved it or not. *"Yes, I can measure it with a stopwatch."*

4. Make sure the goal is relevant. *"My goal is relevant to my life because I want to get fitter."*

5. Give yourself a deadline. Be generous and give yourself a little leeway if necessary. *"I will give myself three weeks to achieve this goal."*

---

[55] Boogard, 2021.

Bonus Activity: Learn to Be More Assertive

In order to break out of negative behavioral patterns, you need to be assertive in your relationships. Know that you have the following rights:[56]

1. to judge your own thoughts, emotions, and behavior
2. to choose whether or not you are responsible for solving others' problems
3. to change your mind
4. to say you don't know
5. to act independently of others' approval
6. to be illogical
7. to say you don't understand something
8. to say you don't care.

In order to be more assertive:[57]

1. Use confident, open body language. Stand straight and directly face the person you are speaking to while maintaining eye contact.

2. Determine what you want and don't want and communicate this to the people around you in a calm, respectful manner.

3. Say you "don't do something" instead of giving excuses when you need to say no. For instance, you can say, "I don't go out the weekend before exams." Using the word "don't" show that your refusal is not personal. It is just one of your boundaries.

---

[56] Psychology Tools, n.d.
[57] Family Therapy Institute of Santa Barbara, n.d.

4. Freely assert your physical, mental, and emotional limits. For instance, if someone is standing too close, you might say, "Sorry, but I need a little more physical distance when talking to someone." You can also learn sentences like "I don't like hugs," or "I don't let people look at the contents of my smartphone."

5. Continue to be caring towards others.

6. Understand that they may make countermoves to get you to be unassertive again. Stand by your resolve, and don't give in.

Returning to Claire

Claire ended up loving the writing workshop and joining many more. Everyone was open and non-judgmental when she read her work. The author she admired complimented one of her short stories and helped her publish it. She also received useful feedback, which she used to improve her writing and make it more exciting.

You are now comfortable reframing your thoughts and beliefs and trying out healthy behaviors. It's time to tackle specific issues using CBT techniques. Let's start with anxiety—an issue affecting nearly one in three teens!

Help other teens get back into the driver's seat of their emotions so they can ace their personal, social, and academic goals.

"Thoughts create emotions, emotions create feelings, and feelings create behavior. So it's very important that our thoughts are positive, to attract the right people, events, and circumstances into our lives."
— Avis Williams

You might remember from the introduction that I mentioned that although you can sometimes feel incredibly lonely as a teen, some of the main challenges you feel—stress, the pressure to succeed, and peer pressure—are shared by most people your age.

As a mom of two teens, I have seen how almost from the moment my kids turned 13, they had more trouble calming themselves down, speaking assertively (rather than raising their voices), and keeping anxiety at bay.

You are not the only one and the many conflicting emotions you are feeling are part of growing up and maturing.

One of my main aims in this book is to empower you in the face of all the major challenges you face. When a tense, stressful, or anger-inducing situation arises, a barrage of automatic thoughts can flood through your mind. These thoughts quickly transform into emotions and then, into behaviors.

Unfortunately, when you allow emotions felt "in the heat of the moment" to hold sway, your behaviors can stand in the way of your goals and harm your relationships.

Throughout the book, I have provided you with a host of exercises aimed at boosting your awareness of the signals your body and mind are constantly sending you.

Clenched fists, faster breathing, a flushed feeling... these are all signs you should listen to if you don't want to get caught in a hurricane of stress, anxiety, and anger.

My daughter, Claire, once told me that it was a pity that they don't really teach emotional intelligence at school. CBT is a powerful tool when it comes to displaying this type of intelligence because it enables you to be the master, not the slave, of your emotions.

If this book is shedding light on how to help you regulate your emotions and get on well with others, you can let other teens know that they can be the master, rather than the slave, of how they think, feel, and behave.

By leaving a review of this book on Amazon, you can help other teens proactively manage their emotions instead of becoming a slave to fear, anger, and anxiety.

Simply by telling them how this book helped you and what they can expect to find inside, you'll help them understand that CBT can help them overcome a myriad of obstacles and establish meaningful relationships with others.

Part 2

CBT

For
Specific Condition

Chapter Five

CBT for Stress and Anxiety

"Stress should be a powerful driving force, not an obstacle."

– Bill Phillips

The teen years can be a uniquely stressful time. The American Institute of Stress reports that:[58]

- Gen Z has higher levels of stress compared to other age groups.
- Americans aged 15 to 29 and 30 to 49 have the highest stress levels in the nation (64 percent and 65 percent, respectively).

Why Are Teens So Stressed?

Many teens feel stressed owing to:

- school frustrations and demands
- negative thoughts or feelings about themselves
  bodily changes taking place

---

[58] The American Institute of Stress, n.d.

- problems with classmates and friends
- living in an unsafe place
- the separation or divorce of parents
- chronic illness or severe problems in the family
- the death of a loved one
- moving or changing schools
- having too many activities going on
- exceedingly high expectations
- having unrealistic expectations because they may compare themselves with Instagram and TikTok influencers
- money problems at home

Malia's Story

Malia is a 17-year-old student in her final year of high school. She is a good student, but she arrived in the US from another country when she was 16, and had to work very hard to catch up with other students (since her curriculum abroad was different).

She started her first year with many Bs and a few Cs in her report card, but has lifted her grade to As for most of her subjects. She still has a couple of subjects she finds challenging (including math, which she was way behind in when she arrived).

Malia studies for hours every day, sometimes conducting detailed research—the kind that is great for class discussions, but which sometimes takes over time she needs to dedicate to math. She worries about upcoming exams and often stays up late, cramming in last minute information. She gets tummy aches and lives off endless cups of coffee, arriving to exams after barely having slept more than five hours.

Teen Anxiety and Depression

Teens have a high level of anxiety. In the US, anxiety and depression are major problems for 70 percent of teens and minor problems for 26 percent of them.

We spoke before of the "fight or flight" response. When you are under its throes, your heart rate rises, you begin breathing in more rapidly, and you can enter into a state of panic.

The good news is that you can turn the stress response off easily through techniques like breathing. By eating regular meals, sleeping eight to ten hours nightly, honing the basics of time management, and developing assertive communication skills, you can greatly reduce your symptoms of stress and anxiety.

How Can CBT Help?

CBT can help the negative, worry-filled cycles that lead to anxiety and

panic. There are useful and unuseful ways to deal with a situation. In previous chapters, you saw how the way you think about situations can improve or worsen their effect on the way you feel and the things you do.[59]

For instance, if a friend stops hanging out with you, you can feel lonely, sad, and tired, and this can stop you from doing more things outside your home and making new friends. You can become trapped in negativity, sitting alone, listening to sad songs, and feeling sorry for yourself.

What if, however, you could accept that friendships don't always last forever, learn from your mistakes, and move on? This simple realization can make you feel much more optimistic, and you can become more socially active and make a new circle of friends.

---

[59] NHS, n.d.

CBT can also help you with anxiety by helping you deal with stress and stop anxiety in its tracks before it manifests itself in panic or other harmful or futile behaviors. If your anxiety is so strong that it interferes with your daily life, however, you can benefit from seeking professional help. One of the gold standard therapies for anxiety is CBT, so you will already have a head start if you are recommended this treatment.

Below are a series of exercises that may also help you see how your thoughts, emotions, and behaviors can make anxiety better or worse.

CBT Exercises for Anxiety

Exercise One: What Could Happen vs. What Will Happen

When something is causing you to stress or worry, it is easy to imagine that the worst thing possible will happen. In reality, things don't often go totally awry. This exercise can open your mind to a more positive way of thinking about these situations.[60]

Fill in the following table:

What Could Happen vs. What Will Happen	
What is something that you are worried about?	Example: I am worried that my whole class will laugh when they see me in shorts for P.E.
List some signs that your worry will not come true.	Teens of all shapes and sizes wear shorts at school for P.E. class and nobody picks on them. Also, the kids in my P.E. class happen to be pretty cool.

---

[60] Therapist Aid, n.d.

If your worry doesn't come true, what will probably happen in its place?	Everyone will probably just play basketball as usual, and I could score a three-pointer like last time.
If your worry does come true, how will you respond?	I would ask them to stop and, if they persisted, inform the teacher.
After answering the above questions, do you view your worry differently?	I am not as worried as I was, because I can see that even in the worst case scenario, I can deal with this problem maturely and not allow it to get me into an anxious state.

YOUR TURN!

What is something that you are worried about?	
List some signs that your worry will not come true.	

If your worry doesn't come true, what will probably happen in its place?	
If your worry does come true, how will you respond?	
After answering the above questions, do you view your worry differently?	

Exercise Two: Anxious Feeling Patterns

In this exercise, you will go back to the essentials of CBT and identify a few of the most common patterns that lead you to feel anxious.[61]

Anxious Feeling Patterns

Trigger or problem:	Example: I have to spend time at my dad's this weekend and I can't stand his new girlfriend.
Thoughts:	Dad is going to make me go out with them to dinner with him and his girlfriend and I feel guilty going because I know how sad my mom is that my dad left her for his new girlfriend.
Feelings:	I feel guilty, frustrated, and sad.
Behavior:	I lash out at my dad and tell him I'm not going.
Consequences:	I am losing the close relationship I had with my dad.

YOUR TURN!

Trigger or problem:	
Thoughts:	

---

[61] University of Washington, n.d.

Feelings:	
Behavior:	
Consequences:	

Exercise Three: Scheduling Your Worry Time

One of the worst things about anxiety is that it can creep up on you when you least expect it. This exercise aims to put you back in the driver's seat by scheduling in time for your worries. Allow yourself 10 minutes to worry (use a stopwatch or timer for this purpose). If worries pop up during other times of the day, remind yourself that you have to save them for your scheduled worry time and think of something else in the meantime.[62]

---

[62] University of Washington, n.d.

Scheduling Your Worry Time

DAY	Scheduled Worry Time 1	Scheduled Worry Time 2	Alternative thoughts and behaviors I used when I was not on "worry time"
Ex. Monday	3pm	7pm	I thought about the interesting concepts in a book I was reading. I went for a run. I focused on my breathing.
Monday			
Tuesday			
Wednesday			
Thursday			
Friday			
Saturday			
Sunday			

Exercise Four: Worry Coping Activities

Choose from one of the activities listed below when you find anxious thoughts racing through your head:[63]

Stop and Listen
Pause whatever you are doing and listen to the surrounding sounds. What can you hear? Are there leaves rustling in the wind? Can you hear a dog barking in the distance? Or cars passing by? Opening your senses up to the "here and now" is a powerful and instant way to escape from the type of thoughts that can cause anxiety and panic.

Talking About It
If you are worried about a specific thing, talk to a trusted parent, sibling, or friend.

Draw Your Worry
Giving shape to your worries can help you recognize them, then let them go. A few ideas for your drawings include:
- Draw what you look like when you're relaxed, and when you're worried.
- Draw something or someone that calms you down when you're worried.
- Draw the thing that is worrying you.

Don't worry if you don't have advanced drawing skills. Studies have shown that creating art is a powerful way to stop stress in its tracks, even if you are an absolute beginner (Hill, 2016).

Diffusing Essential Oils
Studies have shown that essential oils like lavender, ylang ylang, and bergamot lower stress and anxiety levels, blood pressure, heart rate, and stress hormone levels (Healthline, 2022). Invest, if you can, in an essential oil diffuser and make sure that the oils you use are therapeutic-grade. Diffuse these beautiful-smelling oils in your room or your favorite indoor relaxation spot.

Writing a Happy Ending
When you worry a lot, you tend to imagine that things will turn out badly. Write a short story about your worry and write a happy ending. You may write that your worry will become weaker, the situation you worry about won't happen, or you will find a way to deal with whatever the result is.

Traveling With Your Mind
Many people have a bucket list of places they would love to visit. Make a list of your own, then choose one destination. Write down what the place looks, sounds, and feels like, including lots of little details. In your dream getaway, are you eating something scrumptious, hearing someone sing, or touching something soothing—like sand or smooth pebbles?

---

[63] Therapist Aid, n.d.

Exercise Five: Positive Self-Talk

This exercise aims to get you in the habit of saying positive things to yourself, so you can avoid triggering the fight or flight response.[64]

Positive Self-Talk

Fill in the following blanks:

I am worried _
_ _will happen.

> Once you have completed part 1., ask yourself if there is another way you can think about it:

I can do this to make this less worrisome:
_ _
_ _

I can do this now to make myself feel better:
_ _
_ _

> Create a plan: Change your negative self-talk into positive self-talk:
> _
> _

Examples for #1-3:

1. *I am worried that my parents will no longer be able to afford my horse-riding classes.*

---

[64] University of Washington, n.d.

2. I can offer to mow my neighbors' lawns to be able to afford lessons once a week.

3. I'm going to start making flyers offering my services to neighbors my parents approve of. I will run my ideas for making money by my parents first, so I can make sure I'm safe. They may have additional ideas for me or know someone who needs a person to help them out or run errands for them.

Exercise Six: Creating an Exposure Hierarchy

This exercise is arguably one of the most challenging and effective you could try out. This is because it encourages you to "take the anxiety monster by the horns" instead of escaping it. Exposure is a technique that is used to fight avoidance. During exposure, you face trauma reminders in a safe, controlled manner. The aim of this therapy is to show you that things are not as scary as they seem, even though the fight or flight response sometimes tricks you into thinking they are.[65]

Examples of Exposure Activities

The list of things that make each of us worried or anxious can vary greatly. For some people, the following activities can amount to exposure:[66]

- listening to music that reminds them of something traumatic
- writing about a traumatic event
- talking about a traumatic event
- wearing something (for instance, a jewelry item) that reminds you of your trauma
- watching a film that reminds them of their trauma
- reading a true story on Reddit of someone who has experienced similar trauma
- drawing images that remind them of their trauma

---

[65] University of Washington, n.d.
[66] Therapist Aid, n.d.

Choose Trauma Activities That Are:

1. **Safe:** The activities may be uncomfortable, but they should not pose a risk to your safety, health, or well-being.

2. **Controllable:** You should be able to control everything involved in your chosen exposure. For instance, "Watch news about a school threat near me" or "Sit at home and watch the lighting and thunder from indoors" cannot be one of your chosen activities because they are not within your control.

3. **Specific:** Try to indicate your exact plan, so you can prepare for it.

4. **Repeatable:** Every trauma activity you select should be capable of being completed at least four times.

Worksheet

Create an exposure hierarchy, ranking the things that cause you distress. Rate each activity from 1 to 10.

Activity	Distress Rating 1-10
Example: Going to a dog park.	7

Exercise Seven: Interoceptive Exposure Activities

Interoceptive exposure therapy is sometimes used to treat panic and anxiety disorders and phobias. It involves exposing you to the bodily sensations you typically experience when anxiety hits. The idea is that if you can feel these uncomfortable sensations but see that they are not ultimately harmful, you are less likely to get anxious when they arise.

Interoceptive exposure activities include:[67]

- running up a hill until you feel your heart rate rise and you are out of breath
- spinning around while standing on a safe surface (like grass) until you feel dizzy
- breathing fast and deeply
- tensing up the different muscles in your body
- stay in a hot room until you feel sweaty

It is a good idea to get the okay of a professional for these exercises, as they can provoke discomfort.

---

[67] Ackerman, 2017.

Exercise Eight: Functional Analysis Worksheet

Functional Analysis Worksheet

It aims to help you discover more about the causes and effects of your behavior. Knowing this information can help you decide on a healthier behavior next time. Fill in the following table:

Behavior— What was the behavior?	Antecedents— What factors preceded the problematic behavior?	Consequences —What was the result of the problematic behavior?	New behavior— What behavior can I demonstrate next time the teacher announces exams?
Example: I stared hyperventilating in class.	Example: The teacher told us there would be an exam in two weeks.	Example: I felt tired after the panic attack and was not able to study because I felt blocked.	Example: I can immediately start belly breathing to stop my heart rate and breathing rate from rising.

Holistic and Mindfulness Exercises for Anxiety

Mindful exercises are also proven and effective means of reducing the symptoms of anxiety, depression, anger, social anxiety, and other common problems. You should therefore aim to include mindfulness practice in your daily life.

Do so by embracing the following exercises:

Exercise One: The RAIN Mindfulness Exercise

This mindful practice helps you focus on the present and reduce the impact of negative thoughts and emotions.[68]

1. **R**ecognize your thoughts, feelings, and physical sensations. Write down or say the emotion you are experiencing.

2. **A**llow your thoughts, emotions, and sensations to come and go without trying to push them away. Avoid judging yourself or your emotions. Tell yourself, "This is what is going on right now."

3. **I**nvestigate the way that your body is experiencing these emotions. This is also the time in which to investigate the most vulnerable parts of yourself that need love and acceptance.

4. **N**urture yourself by telling yourself something positive such as "I love you," or "I accept you." Think of someone you love or a beloved pet and imagine their love surrounding you like a cloud. Let in healing and compassion until you feel a welcome sense of peace.

---

[68] Therapist Aid, n.d.

Exercise Two: The 5-4-3-2-1 Technique

This is another exercise that grounds you to the present moment in a very pleasant way.[69]

Name:

- 5 things you can see
- 4 things you can feel
- 3 things you can hear
- 2 things you can smell
- 1 thing you can taste

5 things you can see	
4 things you can feel	
3 things you can hear	
2 things you can smell	
1 thing you can taste	

---

[69] Therapist Aid, n.d.

Exercise Three: Mindful Exercise Using a Script

You can record yourself saying the following script, or choose a loved one to record it for you. Play it to yourself and follow its instructions for a quick but effective meditation session.

Practice script:

> Find a comfortable place to lie down or sit. Close your eyes and take a few deep breaths, allowing your body to relax.
>
> Notice the sensations in your body. Feel the weight that your body is placing on the item you are sitting or lying on. Try to notice any part of your body with tense muscles. Don't try to do anything just yet. Simply observe.
>
> Next, do a few belly breaths, allowing yourself to be "in the here and now," letting go of thoughts of the past or future.
>
> If you notice any thoughts or feelings, acknowledge them and eventually allow them to float away like a cloud on a windy day.
>
> Keep breathing for as long as you like, immersing yourself in an ever-deeper state of calm. When you are ready to end this exercise, open your eyes.

Exercise Four: Progressive Muscle Relaxation

Lie down in a comfortable spot and tense one muscle group at a time, then relax it. Start with your toes and end with your face. You can use a YouTube video, an audio recording, or your own mind to practice this technique. Calm and Headspace are two marvelous apps with more mindfulness exercises than you could possibly get through!

Time Management Tips

Managing your time is vital when you have a stressful schedule or you are battling anxiety. Prioritizing activities and sticking to a routine can stop you from feeling like you have too many tasks left and too little time to complete them.[70]

1. Write down your schedule. This is especially important during exam time.

2. Develop routines.

3. Set a personal limit for screen time use.

4. Set goals and break them down into smaller chunks, determining a deadline for achieving each goal.

5. Prioritize more important activities when you have many things to do. You may have to eliminate less crucial activities from your schedule for the time being.

Sleep Can Make or Break Your Report Card

Getting good sleep is one of the most essential things you can do if you have anxiety. Poor sleep can cause you to have a lower tolerance to stress. For starters, you should aim to sleep for eight to ten hours nightly. Bear in mind that sleep quantity is only one-half of a good night's sleep. You also need to ensure you have good sleep quality.

The National Sleep Foundation states that to get good quality sleep, you have to ace the following categories:[71]

1. **Sleep Latency:** This refers to how fast you fall asleep. You should aim to fall asleep within half an hour of getting into bed.

---

[70] Morin, 2019.
[71] The National Sleep Foundation, 2020.

2. **Sleep Waking:** You should wake up no more than once after falling asleep.

3. **Wakefulness:** If you wake up during the night, you should not be awake for longer than 20 minutes in total.

4. **Sleep Efficiency**: This is the amount of time you are actually sleeping when you are in bed. The measurement should be 85 percent or more if you want to wake up feeling refreshed and renewed.

Returning to Malia

Malia felt that she had discovered a whole new world when a teacher organized a mindfulness session for her class. The calm and peace she felt during and after the session led her to research into mindfulness, download apps, and find excellent mindfulness audios and YouTube videos.

She soon had a list of favorite exercises and practiced them every day. She knew some scripts by heart, so when she would feel tense at school, she would find a quiet spot and go through the script to calm her heart rate and keep her emotions in check.

Stress and anxiety can be debilitating, but so can depression, which can take the fun out of life and can stop you from interacting with and enjoying your friends, classmates, and family members to the full. In the next chapter, you will find CBT activities that are specifically aimed at people battling depression.

Chapter Six

CBT for Depression

"I am bent, but not broken. I am scarred, but not disfigured. I am sad, but not hopeless. I am tired, but not powerless. I am angry, but not bitter. I am depressed, but not giving up." — **Anonymous**

Stella's Story

Stella is a teen I know who was in therapy for depression. She had lost her mother to a swift and relentless disease, and Stella began experiencing complicated grief. This type of grief is an ongoing, heightened state of mourning that stops people from healing. Stella felt intense pain and could not stop crying or thinking about her mom for over a year.

She found it hard to concentrate at school or do the things she used to enjoy with her friends. Family and friends tried to help her, but she just wanted to be alone. She thought that life would never be the same until, through therapy, she discovered that she could find its meaning in her loss (Mayo Clinic, n.d.).

Depression and Teens

Depression is a major issue, impacting some 20 percent of adolescents before adulthood and between 10 and 15 percent of people in this age group at any given time.[72] The risk factors for depression include:

- Having experienced abuse or neglect.

---

[72] Mayo Clinic, n.d.

- Having a family history of depression or mental illness.

- Having untreated substance abuse or mental health issues.

Many experts believe that depression rates have risen over the years because of the many pressures teens are subjected to. As mentioned above, many kids are worried about their family's financial problems, as well as academic, social, and family pressures.

Depression Should Be Taken Seriously and Professionally Treated

The activities included here are in no way meant to replace therapy. Depression is a serious matter, and it should be diagnosed and treated. Consider this chapter to be complementary, as it is for other conditions mentioned in Part II of this book.

How Is Teen Depression Treated?

There is no "one-size-fits-all" solution for depression. Some doctors recommend a combination of talk therapy/psychotherapy and medication, though in some cases, they recommend psychotherapy alone, undertaken alone or with other family members.

Through psychotherapy, teens can:

- discover the causes of depression
- learn how to identify and make changes in their thoughts or behaviors
- explore their relationships and experiences
- find effective ways to deal with problems
- set positive, realistic goals for themselves
- feel happy and in control of their thoughts and emotions once again

- feel less hopeless and angry
- adjust to current life challenges

CBT Activities for Depression

Below are a few CBT activities and worksheets that are used to help people get through difficult times.

Exercise One: Control-Influence-Accept

The Control-Influence-Accept Model was first developed by y Neil and Sue Thompson in their book, The Critically Reflective Practitioner. Their research showed them that people who feel depressed often experience:

1. a loss of control
2. indecision

They, therefore, came up with the Control-Influence-Accept model, which can help people deal with an overwhelming situation more productively. The model consists of three elements:[73]

Control:

- your behavior surrounding the event
- when you undertake specific tasks
- your approach to situations and tasks

Influence:

- how you respond to a situation or event
- how you respond to others

---

[73] Thompson & Thompson, 2018.

- knowing who to go to for help or advice

Accept:

- other people's responses or decisions
- the constantly changing world around you

To complete the exercise using this model, take your journal and answer the following:

1. What situation or event made me feel this way?

   Example: My good friend moved to another city.

2. What aspects of the situation or event can I control?

   a. *Example: I can still keep in touch with her via Skype and text.*

   b. _____

   c. _____

3. What can I influence?

   a. *Example: I can talk to her mom and ask her if my friend can visit me for a couple of weeks in the summer.*

   b. _____

   c. _____

   d. _____

   e. _____

4. What do I need to accept?

    a. *Example: My best friend will not always be around as she once was.*

    b. _____

    c. _____

    d. _____

    e. _____

After answering these questions, reflect on the following:

1. How do I feel about the situation after completing this exercise?

   Example: I understand that it is something I just need to accept.

2. Is there anything in #4 That I wish I could control? Why do I feel this way?

   I wish I could have convinced my best friend to stay. I feel this way because I don't have many other friends, and I am scared to look for other people I can trust and get close to.

When completing this exercise, it helps to think of the serenity prayer by American theologian Reinhold Niebuhr.[74] It reads,

"God, grant me the serenity to accept the things I cannot change,

courage to change the things I can,

and wisdom to know the difference."

This poem can be helpful even if you are not religious. It stresses the importance of accepting that some things are beyond your control and that these are the things you inevitably have to accept.

Exercise Two: Finding Alternative Solutions for Guilt

People with depression are more prone to experiencing emotions that are related to self-blame, such as guilt and shame. However, these emotions can drive you further into depression if they are unhelpful. It is, therefore, important to identify patterns of unhelpful guilt or shame. This exercise can help with this task.[75]

Before starting, it helps to differentiate between helpful and unhelpful guilt and to know exactly what shame is. Helpful guilt can arise when you feel bad about something you did that is objectively wrong.

- For example: If I was mean to my younger brother today, I can feel guilty about this and use this guilt to do something good like spend extra time with him, say sorry, and try not to let my anger out on him in the future.

---

[74] Alcoholics Anonymous, n.d.
[75] Pulcu et al., 2013.

Unhelpful guilt is when you feel uncomfortable with something you have done that goes against your standards or values. This type of guilt can be disproportionate, irrational, or misplaced.[76] It sometimes arises when you don't actually have any control over the situation. When you experience this type of guilt, you can resort to self-punishing behaviors.

- For example: I feel guilty because I got a student prize, and my best friend worked harder for it than I did.

Shame is a deeply held belief about your worth. It makes you feel that others would reject you and can cause you to disconnect from them.

- For example: I am ashamed of the area where I live. A couple of kids at school have made fun of me because of it.

Now you are ready to start the exercise.

1. Does your depression make you feel guilty? If so, list this down alongside any other thoughts or reasons for guilt.

   Example: I feel guilty that I'm depressed because I know my parents want me to be happier.

2. Use the following chart to link your guilty thoughts to your sense of self-worth.

---

[76] Mind Tools, n.d.

Finding Alternative Solutions for Guilt

Guilty Thought	Self-Worth
For example: I feel terrible that my siblings have to see me struggling against depression.	For example: I am not a good big brother.

Next, aim to find positive ways to combat your depression by filling in the following blanks:

1. I feel guilty because_____

   Example: I feel guilty because I am often feeling too low to take my little sister to play outside.

2. How do I see myself as a result of these feelings?

   _____

   Example: I see myself as a terrible older brother.

3. A more positive way I can see this is

   _____

   Example: I do my best to let my siblings know I love them, and when my energy levels are high enough, I always give them my time because I am a person of great worth.

Exercise Three: The ABCDE Model

This model can be traced back to the work of American psychologist Albert Ellis in the 1950s. He believed that the treatments available for depression during that time focused too much on past events rather than current beliefs (such as the belief that one is unworthy of love). He came up with a model that links:

- **A**ctivating Events

- **B**eliefs

- **C**onsequences

He called this the ABC Model. It espouses that external events (A) do not cause emotions (C). However, our beliefs (B) do have emotional consequences (C). The model also argues that the type of belief we hold matters and that we can change our beliefs. The main goal of the ABC model is to know how to differentiate between rational and irrational beliefs.[77]

Subsequently, the ABC Model was amplified into the ABCDE Model. It is similar but a little more detailed.

It looks something like this:

- **a**ctivating events
- **b**eliefs about the event
- the emotional **c**onsequences
- **d**isputing irrational beliefs
- **e**ffective new beliefs replace irrational ones

Are you ready to complete the ABCDE Model exercise? Let's get right to it, then.

---

[77] Selva, 2018.

The ABCDE Model

Activating Event	Example: I was the slowest in track today.
Irrational Belief	Example: I'm hopeless. I'm a terrible runner.
Consequence	Example: I felt unmotivated to keep running.
Disputing the Irrational Belief	Example: Two weeks ago, I trained before the race and came third. I can continue doing the same so my time improves.
Effect of the New Rational Belief	Example: I feel better and more positive about my progress in running and I will train harder to get even better at my favorite sport.

YOUR TURN!

Activating Event	
Irrational Belief	
Consequence	
Disputing the Irrational Belief	
Effect of the New Rational Belief	

Exercise Four: Positive Daily Affirmations

You may have read a little about positive daily affirmations or seen your favorite TikTok or Instagram influencers share a few. Telling yourself you are wonderful can seem strange but know that there is a genuine theory and a great deal of neuroscience that backs the validity of this practice.

Many studies show that we can maintain our sense of self-integrity by telling ourselves positive things.[78] Self-affirmation theory has three main ideas behind it:

1. Through self-affirmation, we keep up a narrative about ourselves in which we are flexible, moral, and capable of adapting to different circumstances.

2. Maintaining a positive self-identity is not about being perfect. It is more about being adequate in the specific areas we value.

3. We use positive affirmations not because we want to receive praise but rather because we want to deserve it by behaving in accordance with specific values.

The Benefits of Daily Affirmations

Self-affirmations have been shown to:

- reduce stress
- make us less likely to ignore harmful health warnings and more likely to eat fruits and vegetables
- have a positive link to academic achievement
- help reduce rumination (a type of overthinking in which you run through the same thoughts over and over in your head)

---

[78] Moore, 2019.

Daily Affirmations

Are you ready to make daily affirmations to yourself? Below are just a few affirmations for depression, but you can make your own as well:

1 I recognize that my negative thoughts are irrational and I will ditch them.	**2** I embrace all my emotions.
3 I face my days with courage.	**4** This is just one moment in my life.
5 I have depression but it does not define me and I am getting better every day.	**6** Inside me, I feel at peace.
7 I love myself unconditionally.	**8** I let go of the things I cannot change.
9 I will keep my mind exactly where I am.	**10** I am freeing myself of unhelpful guilt and shame.

Exercise Five: Visualization

When you are depressed, you can feel powerless and that nothing you can do will make a difference. Visualization can mentally transport you to a pleasant place or memory—one that makes you feel happy.

This visualization technique is easy but very powerful.[79] Simply sit in a quiet, calm spot and play some relaxing music. Close your eyes and imagine a safe place you would like to visit or have visited before. Think of your five senses (sight, sound, touch, taste, and smell) and write down or simply keep in mind what you notice in as much detail as possible. Allow yourself to visit this spot for around 10 or 15 minutes every day or when you need to.

Exercise Six: Keep a Self-Care Journal

Numerous studies have shown that journaling can reduce stress and anxiety and help people process emotional hardships. Studies have also shown that expressive writing—particularly for those who have been through trauma—improves one's physical and psychological health.[80]

To keep a self-care journal:

1. Set aside 10 or 15 minutes a day to work on your journal.

2. Write down your feelings without judgment. Imagine that you were sharing your thoughts and emotions with your best friend or someone else you deeply trust.

---

[79] Spring Psychology, 2022.
[80] Madel, 2023.

3. Aim to discover vital information about yourself. Ask yourself enlightening questions such as:

- Where is this emotion coming from?
- Is this an authentic threat, or is this just anxiety or negative thinking in action?
- How can I respond in a way that will not harm myself?
- What can I do to progress?

4. Keep a list of things you are grateful for and read the list at the end of your exercise. Examples of things you feel grateful for can include your family, friends, your home, your pets, and TikTok!

Exercise Seven: Five Good Things

Sometimes, it pays to remind yourself that many wonderful things happened during your day. They may be small things, but they are still worthy of gratitude and celebration. For this exercise:[81]

1. Write down five positive experiences that happened to you on a given day.

2. Ask yourself why they happened, why you were grateful for it, and how you can experience this good thing more often.

3. Do this exercise daily for a full week.

---

[81] Therapist Aid, n.d.

Exercise Eight: Harnessing the Power of Protective Factors

There are many factors that can help protect you against the
negative effects of depression. They include:

1. **Social support:** Having people that you can
   ask for help, feeling free to talk about your
   problems, and feeling love and care for
   others (and knowing they love you too).
2. **Coping skills:** Being aware of your emotions
   and handling them well.
3. **Being in good physical health/being
   physically fit:** Exercising regularly, eating
   healthy foods.
4. **Having a sense of purpose:** Being involved
   meaningfully in education, helping your
   parents and siblings out, and similar.
5. **Having a healthy self-esteem:** Believing you
   have value, accepting your flaws or
   weaknesses, believing that you can learn
   valuable things from mistakes, and believing
   that you can overcome challenges.
6. **Embracing healthy thought processes:** Not
   overthinking things, knowing your strengths
   and weaknesses, and not allowing irrational
   thoughts to have power over you.

Now it's time to pull out your journal and fill in the following table:

Which of the protective factors in 1. to 6. has been most useful to you in difficult times?	Example: 3.—doing exercise regularly.
How have you used this protective factor?	Example: When I was feeling sad and stressed, I went out for a run and took a shower. I felt much more positive and energized.
Name two protective factors you would like to improve.	Example: 1. And 5.
How would life be different if you improved these protective factors?	Example: I would call a friend and do something fun instead of feeling sorry for myself at home (1.) and I would be able to handle disappointments better, without feeling like I'm drawing in guilt and/or shame (5.).
List specific steps that will enable you to use these protective factors to your advantage.	Example: For 1., I will: • Make a plan with friends this weekend. • Call an old friend I have not seen in a while. For 5., I will: • Recognize the things I am good at.

YOUR TURN!

Which of the protective factors in 1. to 6. has been most useful to you in difficult times?	
How have you used this protective factor?	
Name two protective factors you would like to improve.	
How would life be different if you improved these protective factors?	
List specific steps that will enable you to use these protective factors to your advantage.	

Returning to Stella

Stella's therapist suggested CBT as a way for her to understand the relationship between her thought patterns, emotions, and behaviors. Stella used a journal to list down triggering events and to see how she often felt worse than she needed to because she was applying negative filters to situations. For instance, she discovered that she tended to give far more weight to others' negative opinions and to think they were being untruthful or simply trying to be kind when they told her good things about herself. She worked on her self-esteem by embracing a set of strategies that included working out every day, self-affirmations, and writing down the positive things that she had experienced every day.

Remember: If you are struggling with severe symptoms of depression or suicidal thoughts, call the following number in your respective country:

USA: National Suicide Prevention Hotline at 988

UK: Samaritans hotline at 116 123

Australia: Suicide Call Back Service 1300 689 467

Stress, anxiety, and depression are three issues that can interfere with your physical and mental health and well-being. You now know important means through which to pulverize them out of your life. Now it's time to get to one area that may have been causing a bit of grief in your life: Anger Management!

Chapter Seven

CBT for Anger Management

"Holding on to anger is like grasping a hot coal with the intent of throwing it at someone else; you are the one who gets burned." – **Buddha**

Mariam's Story

Mariam was a high school student who was accepting of others and willing to go the extra mile for everyone. She had trouble setting her limits and often acceded to doing things for others, even when it was causing her stress and fatigue. She sometimes felt angry at friends who continually asked for favors.

She felt that they were taking advantage of her. She would simmer for days until a small trigger would result in an angry outburst. She would often take it out on her family, raising her voice, throwing her notebooks across the room, and crying. She desperately wanted to control her emotions, but she felt totally powerless against her rage.

As I mentioned in Chapter 1, almost one in five teens has trouble managing their anger. Moreover, nearly one in every twelve teens has an anger disorder. A study by Harvard Medical School has shown that

"Intermittent explosive disorder" is actually one of the most common mental health disorders in adolescents.[82]

Anger Is Not the Enemy

Anger is not a negative emotion. It is what you do with it that turns it into a positive or negative force.

Anger deserves your attention and respect. It can be a sign that you need to change something in your life, that you need to set boundaries with others, or that you need to exercise more self-care.

As stated by Psychologist Dr. Harriet Lerner, anger has two important functions:[83]

- It helps us define ourselves.
- It is a vehicle for personal, social, and political change.

Lerner says, "The pain of our anger preserves the dignity of the self. In other words, when you are feeling angry, that is probably a sign that there is someplace where you are ignoring your needs and betraying yourself."

When you deny, silence, or vent your anger in a way that makes you feel powerless and helpless, this emotion becomes useless. Indeed, it can cause great harm to yourself and your relationships.

Anger can also be pointless if you don't use it to its best benefit. This may be the case if you:

- get angry to blow off steam but don't make positive changes
- avoid conflict at all costs, bottling your anger inside

---

[82] Kotz, 2012.
[83] Sattin, 2015.

Why Is Anger Sometimes Hard to Manage?

Anger is a challenging emotion because human beings are wired for fight or flight. In order to turn anger into something useful, we need to nip this response in the bud and put on our thinking caps.

The Cycle of Anger

For CBT purposes, it pays to understand the cycle of anger. This cycle goes through five stages:

1 A triggering event happens. Example: Someone tailgates you when you're driving.

2 Negative thoughts arise. Example: That driver has no human decency and is selfish.

3 You have an emotional response. Example: You can feel furious at the other driver.

4 Physical symptoms. Example: Your heart races, and you feel tension in your shoulders, neck, and face.

5 Behavioral response: You can shout at the driver or make them an angry gesture.

What Are the Steps Involved in Emotional Regulation for Anger?

Emotional regulation involves managing your emotions, so you can obtain a positive outcome. You can effectively manage your anger by doing the following:

1. Notice and recognize your anger. Signs that you are getting angry include:

   o a racing heart rate
   o feeling flushed
   o feeling defensive about things

2. Deal with the emotion. When you feel angry, you have various ways of dealing with it. For instance, you may:

   o Take a break.
   o Practice belly breathing and calming down.

3. Make a plan for change. If certain situations continually trigger your anger, you can reduce their ability to affect your peace of mind by:

   o Assertively set limits and say no when you need to.
   o Avoid harmful triggers. For instance:

     ▪ If getting in line and waiting for a long time makes you angry, you can plan to visit busy places during off-peak times.

- If you always argue with your sibling in the evening, avoid bringing up difficult points in the evening when you are both tired and are likely to have less patience.

- If you are constantly annoyed that your younger brother takes your things, ask your parents to keep these items in a safe spot when you are not using them.

How Can CBT Help Teens Manage Their Anger?

CBT benefits you in many ways if you want to manage your anger more optimally.[84] It can help you to do the following:

- Understand your triggers for anger.
- Identity unhelpful thought patterns and change inaccurate beliefs.
- Develop and practice coping skills.
- Learn to think, feel, and behave differently in response to anger.
- Gain control over situations.
- Feel more positive.

CBT Exercises for Anger Management

I hope you're inspired to try out a few activities that can help you understand more about how to harness the power of anger to make positive changes in your life.

---

[84] Gupta, 2021.

Exercise One: The Anger Iceberg

The anger iceberg represents the idea that although anger is the emotion you may express externally, there are many emotions that may be hidden beneath the surface—for instance, frustration, guilt, anger, and sadness. These emotions may cause you to feel vulnerable, and if you don't know how to manage them well, the result can be anger.

By exploring other emotions that may be bubbling under the surface, you can take the steps you need to manage them better. For instance, if you are feeling sad because a friend left town, you may need to take steps to expand your friendship circle. If you are feeling neglected by a friend, then working on assertive communication can help you address this problem without blowing your cool.

Let's get to the Anger Iceberg Activity.[85]

The tip of the iceberg which is the behavior you display is Anger but below the surface are the emotions your anger may be masking.

Like the example on the next page.

---

[85] Therapist Aid, n.d.

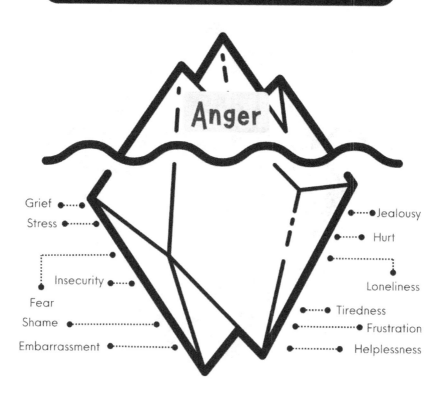

The Anger Iceberg

Anger

Grief
Stress
Insecurity
Fear
Shame
Embarrassment

Jealousy
Hurt
Loneliness
Tiredness
Frustration
Helplessness

Next, think of the last situation that made you angry. Try to think if any of the above emotions were the cause of your anger. Think about your family. Is anger seen as a more acceptable emotion than other emotions?

Try to take action to resolve any emotions that you have not addressed.

YOUR TURN

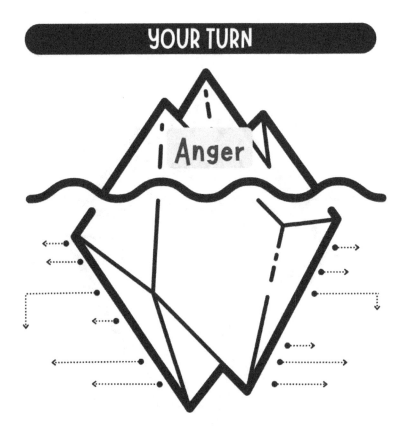

Exercise Two: Know Your Warning Signs

You will have worked out by now that one of the keyways to manage your emotions is to be aware of bodily sensations and automatic thoughts. This exercise is simple, but its significance is deep. Look at this table of clues that your anger is starting to grow. Think about those that apply to you. The next time they happen, remember to address them while they are still weak. You now know many ways to calm your anger.

You might practice belly breathing, go to a green spot for a few minutes, or do some exercise. You can make your own list of tried-and-tested activities that help you go from simmering to cool, so you can think about your problems logically and take strategic actions.[86]

Warning Signs Of Anger

○ Sweating

○ Muscle tightness

○ Not being able to get over a problem

○ Feeling sick in the tummy

○ Feeling hot or turning red

○ Becoming completely quiet

○ Using verbal insults

○ Clenched fists

○ Headaches

[86] Therapist Aid, n.d.

Exercise 3: Anger-Busting Activities

Below is a table with a few anger-busting activities. Circle the ones you think you'd like to try, and the next time you have anger warning signs, schedule at least one of them into your day.[87]

---

[87] Therapist Aid, n.d.

Exercise Four: Recognizing the Effects of Anger

Effects Of Anger

When anger is expressed negatively, it can have an effect on our relationships and our school or work performance. This exercise is geared to help you think about the effect of unleashing unmitigated anger on others (Therapist Aid, n.d.).[85] Answer the following four questions:

How has your anger impacted other people?	Example: I hurt my friend the other day by shouting at her and saying an insult.	To what extent has this posed a problem for you? 1. Not at all 2. A little 3. **A lot**
How has anger affected your performance at school or college?	Example: I got angry while working on a group project and the others don't want to work with me anymore.	To what extent has this posed a problem for you? 1. Not at all 2. A little 3. **A lot**
How has anger impacted your physical or mental health?	Example: I got really angry at my classmate and afterwards, I got a panic attack.	To what extent has this posed a problem for you? 1. Not at all 2. A little 3. **A lot**
Think of a time when your anger was too intense.	Example: I found out that a friend had been criticizing me to others. I was driving her home from a party and I unleashed my fury on her, shouting and driving fast. I had to brake very suddenly when another car braked in front of me. It was scary as we almost got into an accident.	To what extent has this posed a problem for you? 1. Not at all 2. A little 3. **A lot**

YOUR TURN!

How has your anger impacted other people?		To what extent has this posed a problem for you? 1. Not at all 2. A little 3. A lot ------------------
How has anger affected your performance at school or college?		To what extent has this posed a problem for you? 1. Not at all 2. A little 3. A lot ------------------
How has anger impacted your physical or mental health?		To what extent has this posed a problem for you? 1. Not at all 2. A little 3. A lot ------------------
Think of a time when your anger was too intense.		To what extent has this posed a problem for you? 1. Not at all 2. A little 3. A lot ------------------

Exercise Five: Know Your Triggers

The things that trigger anger are very individual. They vary considerably from person to person. They include people, situations, behaviors, thoughts, and emotional states. Before starting this exercise, think about the things that make you angry.[88]

Examples:

- feeling tired
- rude, inconsiderate drivers on the road to school/college
- not getting enough sleep
- too much schoolwork
- disloyal behavior from friends
- when I don't exercise and get out of shape

Now it's time to work in more detail!

1. Write down your three strongest triggers.
2. Write down one strategy for avoiding or reducing your exposure to these triggers.
3. Write down one strategy for dealing with these triggers if they are unavoidable.

Example:

1. My three strongest triggers are:

    a. Not getting enough sleep.
    b. Not being trusted by a friend.
    c. Having too much work.

---

[88] Therapist Aid, n.d.

2. To avoid these triggers, I can:

    a. Establish a sleep routine and turn off my screens about an hour before I sleep.

    b. Talk to my friend about how trust is very important to me, or spend more time with friends who trust me and less or no time with those who have shown mistrust time and time again.

    c. Try to reduce the amount of work I have by taking on fewer optional subjects.

3. If I can't avoid these triggers, I can:

    a. There is no getting around this. I need sleep and must find a way to get it. To do so, I will have to do things like cut down my screen time, reduce the number of extracurricular activities I do, or similar.

    b. If my friend continues to mistrust me, I may have to end the friendship.

    c. Manage my time better and start working on projects and studying for exams according to a schedule. This way, I work in chunks instead of leaving it all to the end and allowing things to get the better of me.

Exercise Six: Mindfulness Exercise for Anger

Mindfulness is a great tool to have around when you are angry because it enables you to recognize your emotions without letting them control your actions. In this exercise, you will be focusing on your bodily sensations and the messages they are giving you.[89]

1. Find a relaxing, quiet spot in your home or in a park or garden. The seaside is also a great spot for mindfulness exercises.

---

[89] Ineffable Living, 2022.

2. Think about something that made you angry recently. Choose an experience that made you moderately (not extremely) angry.

3. As you focus on this experience, notice the sensations taking place in your body.

4. Scan your entire body, trying to notice areas that feel tense, sweaty, flushed, and similar.

5. If you find yourself judging these sensations, take your mind back to the sensations themselves.

6. Notice any urges your anger brings about and just focus on the emotion without trying to push it out of your mind.

7. Do this for around 15 minutes or until the emotions become less intense.

Exercise Seven: Reflecting on Your Own Role in Angry Incidents

This exercise once again asks you to reflect on a time you were angry, but its focus is on how you may have contributed to the situation.[90]

1. Think back to an unfair situation that made you angry or that stood in the way of your goals.

2. If the situation was not unfair, was there someone standing in the way of your goals?

3. What did anger feel like in your body? Did these sensations help or hinder you in responding to the unfair event?

4. How did you express your anger (verbally and non-verbally)?

5. Could you have done anything that contributed to this situation?

---

[90] Ineffable Living, 2022.

Exercise Eight: Problem-Solving Exercise

Once you know how to keep your anger in check, you may still have a problem to solve. To do so, follow this CBT method:[91]

1. Ask yourself when and where the problem tends to occur.
2. Think about all the causes of your problem.
3. Define the problem.
4. Brainstorm three to five solutions.
5. Weigh the pros and cons of each solution.
6. Choose one solution.
7. Reflect on whether it worked. If it didn't go as well as you thought, try another of the solutions you identified the next time the situation arises.

Exercise Nine: Identifying How Cognitive Distortions Can Make You Angry

In Chapter 2, we spoke of cognitive distortions—the harmful filters that can fuel your anger. The filters that can increase your anger include catastrophizing ("This is going to be the worst experience ever!"), labeling others ("She is so stupid!"), or overgeneralizing ("Bad things always happen to me!").

For this exercise, do the following:[92]

1. Identify the types of situations that make you angry. *Example: I get angry when my friends don't answer my texts quickly.*
2. Identify the harmful filters (or cognitive distortions) you tend to use during these situations. *Example: I sometimes catastrophize:*

---

[91] Huddle IQ, n.d.
[92] Ineffable Living, 2022.

I assume they don't like me, and that is why they didn't answer me.

3. Reflect on what the use of these filters says about you. *Example: I tend to jump to the worst conclusion without the right evidence for it.*

4. Consider your tendency to use these specific filters when you are angry. *Example: I tend to catastrophize or over-generalize when I'm angry.*

5. Try to reappraise the situation by reinterpreting the same event more positively. *Example: Maybe my friend was busy with schoolwork, or maybe they were busy with their parents, and they hadn't seen my text.*

Exercise Ten: Reality Acceptance Skills

This exercise seems simple, but it actually requires discipline and commitment.[93]

When someone says something that hurts you, don't refuse to accept it or ruminate/overthink. Accept that they said something painful. When you have cooled off, think about how to take effective action. For instance, you might calmly tell them that what happened hurt you; listen to their point of view. You should both apologize if you have to and commit to not doing or saying the things that hurt the other person.

Exercise Eleven: Communicating Your Anger in a Healthy Way

When someone does something that makes you angry, talking to them can ensure it doesn't happen again. However, you have to think about what you want to say to ensure you achieve your goal. Follow these steps the next time you need to discuss an anger-provoking situation with someone:[94]

---

[93] Ineffable Living, 2022.
[94] Ineffable Living, 2022.

1. Identify your goal. For example: You might want that person to respect your boundaries.

2. Plan ahead for the conversation. Don't have the talk when you are in the heat of the moment. Think about what they might say when you talk to them about the situation.

3. Practice the following sentence structure: "When X happened, I felt Y." Avoid using "You" statements, like "You always" or "You never." "You" statements make people feel defensive.

4. Stay calm throughout the talk. Don't name-call or raise your voice.

5. Listen openly to their point of view.

6. Take a break if things get heated, and agree to talk again on a future date or time.

Returning to Mariam

Mariam decided to try managing her anger in a way that would help her improve (instead of harm) her relationships. For one, she began to say "no" more often without giving lengthy reasons why she didn't do things others wanted her to. It was not easy at first. When you make positive changes, such as setting your personal limits, the people in your life may try to make you change things back to how they used to be. Mariam knew that if she continued to comply with everyone's demands, however, she would continue feeling exhausted, angry, and abused. She stood her ground, and most of the people in her life accepted and respected her change. A couple abandoned the friendships, but this only made Mariam realize that the only reason they were around her in the first place was to receive favors. She decided she was better off without them.

You now know how to leverage CBT for common mental health challenges and conundrums. If you are shy and would like to be a more confident communicator, then move on to Chapter 8, which will enable you to interact more confidently with others.

Chapter Eight

CBT for Social Anxiety

"Care about what other people think and you will always be their prisoner." – Lao-Tze

Vincent's Story

Vincent was a teen who had social anxiety. He was very shy and hated parties and other social situations in which he had to be around people he didn't know very well. He was always afraid he would say something stupid and that others would laugh at him or judge him.

When he attended social events, he felt totally drained and needed plenty of time alone to recover. He wished he didn't feel that way because he often felt lonely when his best friend was out with other friends. He wished he could build a bigger friend group.

Did you know that social anxiety affects one in three teens? In fact, it is the third most common mental health disorder in the US.[95] There are many reasons why a person might have social anxiety, including genetics and their family environment, and traumatic experiences.

---

[95] Polaris Teen Center, 2019.

What is Social Anxiety Disorder (SAD) or Social Phobia?

Social anxiety disorder or social phobia is a pervasive fear of social interaction and other situations where embarrassment might occur. Its symptoms include:

- anxiety about being with other people (especially new acquaintances)
- difficulty talking to and/or having "normal" conversations
- feeling uncomfortable or self-conscious around other people
- experiencing embarrassment while interacting with others
- fear of being embarrassed
- self-judgment and criticism after social interactions
- fear of being judged by others
- worry for days or weeks before a public event
- avoidance of public places and/or social situations
- difficulty making friends and maintaining relationships
- blushing, sweating, shaking, or rapid heartbeat when in social situations
- physical symptoms such as stomachache, confusion, diarrhea, and muscle tension

CBT for SAD and Improved Communication

CBT is the most used therapy for SAD. However, it can also be used by shy or introverted people who wish to communicate better with others. When used for SAD, CBT consists of:[96]

1. **Cognitive Restructuring:** Reframe your thoughts and beliefs so you see a situation in a more positive light.

---

[96] Cuncic, 2021.

2. **Mindfulness**: Accept emotions and keep the mind "in the here and now."

3. **Behavioral Experiments or Exposures:** Try out experiences you may be uncomfortable with and/or slowly build up your exposure to things you are uncomfortable with.

4. **Assertiveness and Problem-Solving:** Set your boundaries, express your needs and wants assertively, and embrace a sound problem-solving strategy.

5. **Changing Core Beliefs and Personal Rules:** Put an end to destructive beliefs and personal rules that can stand in the way of your happiness.

CBT Activities for Social Anxiety

Below are a few activities that help reduce the symptoms of social anxiety and social shyness. Try out one or more!

Exercise One: Why Work (or Not) on Your Social Anxiety?

The following activity aims to help you understand more about how social anxiety affects your life and the way in which working on it can change your life.[97]

Decision	Pros	Cons
I will work on my social anxiety.	Example: • I will be able to attend more parties. • I can make more friends. • Speaking in front of my class won't be so tough.	Example: • I will have to slowly socialize more, and being around others is currently uncomfortable. • I am scared that I won't succeed.

---

[97] Oxford Clinical Psychology, n.d.

	Example:	Example:
I won't work on my social anxiety and leave things as they are.	• It's easy to sit at home and do nothing. • I won't have to call anyone, go to any parties, or speak in front of the class.	• I will continue to feel lonely. • Sometimes there is no option to be around others and I will continue to feel uncomfortable around them. • If I keep staying home every time I am due to speak before the class, my grades will suffer.

YOUR TURN!

Decision	Pros	Cons

Exercise Two: Monitoring the Components of Your Social Anxiety

This exercise seeks to highlight the link between your thoughts, emotions, and behaviors.[98]

---

[98] Oxford Clinical Psychology, n.d.

Think of a recent social or performance situation that caused you to feel anxious. Example: A classmate's birthday party.

Components		
Physical Signs of Social Anxiety	**Thoughts**	**Behaviors**
Example: palpitations, dizziness, shakiness, flushing/blushing, a lump in my throat.	Everyone thinks I'm a loser or dumb. They're going to laugh at me. I'm scared to eat because I might eat funnily or food might drop from my mouth.	I leave the social occasion. I don't eat any food. I spend ages in the bathroom or a quiet spot in the house, so I don't have to be with anyone.

Think of something positive you can do when these symptoms arise next time. Example: You can start belly breathing, which will bring your heart rate down and stop the "fight or flight" response in its tracks.

Physical Signs of Social Anxiety	Thoughts	Behaviors

Exercise Three: My Fear and Avoidance Hierarchy

To know more about your own anxiety, it helps to create a fear and avoidance hierarchy. This is because when you decide to tackle these issues, you might decide to start with something that causes you less fear (or that you avoid least) and work your way up to more challenging situations.[99]

1. List down the situations that you find difficult. For example:

    a. meeting new people at parties

    b. working in group projects with classmates I don't know well

    c. eating in public

    d. starting a conversation with someone

2. Rate them from 1 to 100 in terms of:

    a. How severe is the anxiety that they provoke?

        1. meeting new people at parties = anxiety score: 85

        2. working in group projects with classmates I don't know well = anxiety score: 70

        3. eating in public = anxiety score: 65

        4. starting a conversation with someone = anxiety score: 90

    b. How often do you avoid the situation?

        1. meeting new people at parties = avoidance score: 90

        2. working in group projects with classmates I don't know well = avoidance score: 50

        3. eating in public = avoidance score: 60

---

[99] Therapist Aid, n.d.

4. starting a conversation with someone = avoidance score: 90

This exercise is useful when you want to start exposing yourself to your fears. Always start with activities with a low avoidance score and build upward. Don't start with something too difficult, or you might be put off from tackling other challenging activities.

Exercise Four: Putting Yourself Back in the Driver's Seat.

Driver's Seat

In this exercise, you will write down a dialogue that will help highlight the fact that you are the boss of your thoughts, not the other way around. The exercise involves writing down one anxious thought and one coping thought

Anxious Thought	Coping Thoughts
I'm going to stumble over words at the party, and they will all laugh at me.	If I stumble over words, I can use humor to get over my tension. I can say something like that, "Oops, my mouth is thinking faster than my brain," or something similar.

Exercise Five: 10 Key Questions

This worksheet invites you to challenge negative thoughts by asking yourself important questions.[100]

10 Key Questions

Beneath each of the 10 Key Questions, write down a triggering situation and the automatic thoughts that arise. Next, answer the question.

1. Am I confusing a thought with a fact?
2. Am I assuming my viewpoint is the only one possible?
3. Am I focusing on my weaknesses and ignoring my strengths?
4. Am I blaming myself for something that is not my fault?
5. Am I taking this personally?
6. Am I only noticing the dark side of things?
7. Am I overestimating the chances of disaster?
8. Am I assuming that there is nothing I can do to change my situation?
9. Am I wishing things were the way they used to be, instead of accepting things as they are?
10. Am I asking questions that have no answers?

Example answer:
1. **Am I confusing a thought with a fact?**
Situation:
    Example: When I saw Sacha at school today, he wasn't as friendly as he usually is.
Automatic thought:
    Example: He must be mad at me.

---

[100] Northeastern Ohio Universities Colleges of Medicine and Pharmacy, n.d.

Exercise Six: Exposing Yourself to Social Situations

Below are five behavioral experiments you might try. They involve exposing yourself to social situations. The more you practice them, the more the tension surrounding the situation can be reduced.[101]

1. Smile and say hi to a classmate or acquaintance you see today.
2. Ask someone for the time.
3. Pay someone a compliment.
4. Make small talk with someone today. It might be at a store, in an elevator, on when you're standing near someone in a line.
5. Call someone from your class to ask about homework or other schoolwork. Try to keep chatting after they share the information you have asked for.

Exercise Seven: Head Held High Assertion

This exercise encourages you to identify and practice what you would say and do if your fears came true. It asks you to come up with a positive assertion that demonstrates that even if the worst thing you could imagine came true, it would not be the end of the world.[102]

What would happen if your worst fear came true?

Example: If I was eating out and a piece of food dropped from my mouth, the other people eating with me would say I was gross.

Head held high assertion: That could happen, but if it does, I could make a joke and say it's really hard to eat with braces. Food accidents

---

[101] Bailey, 2014.
[102] National Social Anxiety Center, n.d.

sometimes happen when you're eating out, and they could happen to anyone.

Example 2: If I was at a party and I made a funny remark, someone would roll their eyes or tell me I was dumb.

Head held high assertion: I could simply find other people who are more empathetic and who like making new people feel at home. Most people try to accept and accommodate others and understand that making small talk can be difficult.

Exercise Eight: Embracing My Fears

This exercise asks you to set exposure goals for yourself. That means doing things that may make you anxious or uncomfortable. You can pick the least difficult of items on this list, working your way up to more challenging ones. You can make it a point to choose one a day or one a week:

1. Focus mindfully on a conversation.
2. Disagree with someone.
3. Walk up to a group of people and join their conversation.
4. Start a conversation with someone.
5. Apply for a job.
6. Attend a job interview.
7. Give an opinion in class.
8. Ask a classmate for help.
9. Tell someone a funny story.
10. Go out to eat with someone or with a group of people.
11. Dance, sing, act, or play a musical instrument before an audience.

You can also set "paradoxical goals" for yourself. These goals set you up for "failure" to make you realize that even your worst fears often never happen. Moreover, if they do, it's not the end of the world.[103]

1. Ask a deliberately "dumb" question.
2. When you're out eating, provoke a mishap (like eating a piece of lettuce that is too large or getting sauce all over your hands).
3. Make yourself seem anxious when talking to others (let your voice quiver, make your hands shake, and similar).
4. Tell someone you are nervous while talking to them.
5. Dress in a funny outfit at the next small party you are invited to.
6. Act clumsy in front of others.
7. Do something annoying.
8. Ask someone for a favor with the goal of being turned down.
9. Make obvious mistakes that people can see.

I know that "paradoxical goal" activities can seem daunting at first, but you may be surprised at how effective they are at making you see the humorous, light, or positive side to situations.

Returning to Vincent

When Vincent turned 15, he got tired of sitting at home by himself. He tried a few paradoxical goals, one of which was asking someone a favor with the goal of being turned down. The funny thing is, the classmate he asked the favor of was glad to help, and they struck up a friendship. Vincent grew more and more confident and started trying out more paradoxical goals. Sometimes, the results were very comical, and he started to enjoy being part of the joke (not the butt of it). He realized that it's okay to be quirky, imperfect, and yourself.

---

[103] Berashat & Naghipoor, 2019.

Chapter Nine

Bonus Activities: NLP and DBT Exercises

"Pessimistic thoughts will only yield trees unwilling to bear edible fruit. Optimistic thinking will always feed those who are willing to sit at your table"."

— *Michaelson Williams*

You have so many CBT exercises in Chapters 1 to 8 that you'll probably be very busy! In this chapter, we will provide activities utilizing two more approaches that are effective for emotional regulation. They are Neurolinguistic Programming (NLP) and Dialectical Behavior Therapy (DBT).

What is NLP?

Neurolinguistic Programming (or NLP) is a different discipline from CBT, but both approaches have important things in common. For instance, NLP and CBT are both centered on changing negative, unhelpful thinking habits. While CBT is mainly used by counselors and hypnotherapists, NLP is more often relied upon by coaches as their preferred mode of therapy.

The cornerstone of NLP is focusing on what we WANT to do instead of what we don't. In other words, you have to get rid of your automatic negative thoughts if you want to move forward.[104]

---

[104] Wyatt, n.d.

NLP Activities for Emotional Regulation

Let's get straight to some NLP activities that will help boost positive thinking and help you deal with tough thoughts and emotions.

Exercise One: Anchoring Emotions

The aim of this exercise is to connect you to a positive state.[105] To anchor your emotions:

1. Think back to a positive emotional state—for instance, feeling happy.

2. Imagine you are back in that state. To boost your imagination, you can visualize a past event that made you happy or imagine a new one that makes you feel positive.

3. Look at what is happening around you when you are in that state.

4. You can access this feeling by connecting it to an "anchor." One typical anchor involves squeezing the tip of your thumb and a finger in a specific way as the feeling builds up, then letting go before the emotion reaches its peak. If you repeat this various times, you can build up an automatic response you can use when you want to feel a positive emotional state again.

Exercise Two: Visualization Exercises

The way you visualize an issue can make it more positive or negative to you. This NLP exercise invites you to improve the way you feel and the results you obtain by making changes in how you visualize a situation.[106]

---

[105] Martins Hervington, 2000.
[106] Martins Hervington, 2000.

Visualization

Visual Feature	Things to Consider
Size	How big is the issue you are visualizing? Reduce the size of the problem by making it "shrink" in size in your head.
Viewpoint	Are you in the image you are visualizing, or are you just an observer? Imagine yourself taking positive control of the situation.
Color	Are you thinking of a task you would like to do in black and white or color? Imagine your goal in vivid colors.
Motion	Is the image you are visualizing static or moving? Is it moving at a normal speed, fast, or slow? Slow down the images when you get to critical issues.
Distance	Bring images closer to you to make them more important, and further away to lessen their importance.
Perspective	Are you seeing things in 2D or 3D? You can feel more motivated by an image if you see it in 3D.

Exercise Three: Meta-Modelling

This is one of the most powerful NLP techniques, and you may find that it has a lot in common with CBT. Its aim is to look at the language you use in everyday life and to pay attention to three types of patterns: [107]

1. **Generalizations:** This includes thoughts like "Bad things always happen to me." "People don't like me." or "All men/women are the same."
2. **Distortions:** We have covered distortions extensively in previous chapters. Some of the most common include jumping to negative conclusions and overgeneralizing.
3. **Deletions:** Deletions involve cherry-picking your understanding of reality, so it fits in with your core beliefs. For instance, if you have low self-esteem and someone compliments you, you may ignore the compliments and pay much more attention to other people's criticisms.

When you have negative thoughts, consider if they belong to categories 1, 2, or 3. Question these by asking yourself various questions. For instance, if you find yourself saying, "People think I'm boring," ask yourself, "Who exactly thinks I'm boring?" "How, exactly, do I know this?"

Your answers may have the words "always" or "never" in them. Ask yourself if you are being realistic when you say things are always or never a specific way. Next, ask yourself about alternative courses of action. For instance, if you tell yourself, "If I don't get a good grade on the next test, I'll feel like a failure," ask yourself if feeling like a failure is your only option.

---

[107] Chris, n.d.

Exercise Four: The Swish Pattern

This exercise invites you to change the way you think, feel, and act.

To do this exercise:[108]

1. Find your trigger. The trigger is the thing that starts an unwanted behavior or habit. For instance, if you feel nervous right before an exam, the trigger might be something you saw, heard, or felt.
2. Identify an image in your head with the trigger. For instance, you might imagine yourself sitting in the exam room.
3. Choose an alternative image. Instead of imagining yourself nervous in the exam room, see yourself doing brilliantly. Create an empowering picture.
4. You now have two images to envision: the undesired one and the desired one. Bring the undesired one in front of your mind's eye and make it big and bold. Obtain the desired picture and make it small and dark, keeping it in the bottom left-hand corner of your mind's eye
5. It's time to perform the swish! Switch the position of the images simultaneously with an imaginary "Swish!" At this precise moment, the undesired image will become tiny and move to the bottom left corner of your mind's eye, and the desired picture will move to the center of your mind's eye and become big and bold.

What Is DBT?

You now know that CBT enables you to recognize harmful thoughts and gives you techniques to reframe those thoughts. DBT, or Dialectical Behavior Therapy, is a type of CBT. Its aim is to help you find ways to accept yourself, feel safe, and manage your emotions, so you can regulate your emotions and behaviors.[109]

---

[108] NLP Essential Guide, n.d.
[109] Skyland Trail, 2017.

DBT Exercises for Teens

Below are three DBT exercises that can help you improve your emotional regulation.

Exercise One: Improve the Moment

This exercise helps you get through emotionally trying situations. Make your way through each of the initials in the acronym IMPROVE.[110]

Improve The Moment	
I—Imagery	Imagine a relaxing place you would love to be in. Imagine this place in detail, noticing sights, sounds, smells, tastes, and similar. You can also imagine the best possible solution to your current problem.
M—Meaning	Think of how you can find meaning from a difficult situation. Think of and write down the ways you could grow from this situation.
P—Prayer	Connect with a higher power or your own intelligent mind. You can also say a prayer if you wish.
R—Relaxing Actions	Find a quiet place where you can take part in a relaxing activity like breathing or mindfulness meditation.
O—One thing in the Moment	Do something repetitive. It could be a household chore, or completing a mental task like a difficult multiplication table or memorizing a poem.
V—Vacation	Take a short break from your studies or work and do something that makes you feel refreshed and happy afterwards.
E—Encouragement	Give yourself encouragement with affirmations like "This too will pass." "I've been through this before and I survived it," or "I'll be okay!"

---

[110] Greene, 2020.

Exercise Two: ACCEPTS

The acronym ACCEPTS stands for 7 different things you can do when you are feeling stressed or when you encounter difficult emotions. It stands for:[111]

1. **Activities**—Do an activity that requires your full concentration.
2. **Contributing**—Do something that focuses on someone else (for instance, volunteer work or helping out a friend or family member).
3. **Comparisons**—Compare your situation to a much more difficult one.
4. **Emotions**—Do something new that will compete with your difficult emotion. For instance, if you're anxious, head to a park. If you're angry, work out. If you're sad, watch Napoleon Dynamite's dance on YouTube and try to learn the choreography.
5. **Pushing Away:** Block pain by using techniques such as visualization to reduce its power over you.
6. **Thoughts:** Use thoughts to shift your mind to a more neutral spot. For instance, you might sing a song out loud or take a poem and read it out loud.
7. **Sensations:** Embrace new sensations to enable you to enter a mindful state. For instance, you might bite into something cold, make a hot cup of tea, or take a cold shower.

---

[111] Therapist Aid, n.d.

Exercise Three: The DEAR MAN Technique to Ask for Something You Want

DEAR MAN is another acronym used in DBT. Its aim is to enable you to deal with others effectively and to be able to ask for something or assert yourself. It goes something like this - When a situation arises, you'd like to discuss with someone else:

D	**DESCRIBE** the situation objectively. Stick to the facts and avoid opinions or interpretations. Example: (Talking to your friend, Carlo): "So you want me to go to the Travis Scott concert with you, and I have already told Jen I would be going to her piano concert."
E	**EXPRESS** your feelings clearly. Example: "When I am expected to dump my plans with my other friends, it makes me feel like my relationships with them don't matter."
A	**ASSERT** yourself, without beating around the bush. Example: "I won't be able to go to the Travis Scott concert because I already committed to Jen's piano recital."
R	**REINFORCE** positive behavior. Example: If your friend is understanding about it, you might thank them or say you really appreciate their understanding.
M	**MINDFUL** Stick to the present situation. Don't get sidetracked into harmful arguments, lose focus, or bring up unrelated situations from the past.
A	**APPEAR** confident. Use positive body language and active listening skills.
N	**NEGOTIATE** Be open to compromise. Example: "I can't go to this concert, but I can definitely accompany you to Scott's party next weekend."

I hope you have enjoyed learning two more approaches to a more confident, happier you. You now have so many exercises and activities to try, many of which will take just a few minutes of your day! Try to be consistent with these activities, so you can achieve the progress you desire.

Conclusion

"I learned that courage was not the absence of fear, but the triumph over it. The brave man is not he who does not feel afraid, but he who conquers that fear."

— Nelson Mandela

The teen years are undoubtedly as fun as they are challenging, as promising as they are pressure-filled, and as busy as they are entertaining. I mentioned earlier that many studies have shown that today's teens face far more pressure than their parents or grandparents did.

There is a lot of pressure these days to do well at school, shine in sports, and demonstrate the "soft skills" that teachers and future employers are looking for. Your teachers often say they expect concentration and focus in the classroom, but it can be so difficult to resist the impulse to chat with classmates or to focus for hours on one topic. It can also be challenging to keep your emotions in check, calm yourself down when a tense situation arises, or communicate assertively when emotions like stress or anger take over.

In part, controlling your impulses and managing your emotions is harder when you're a teen because of hormonal surges and the fact that your brain is still maturing.

Having said that, you are not helpless against these phenomena.

Being proactive and managing your emotions well starts by taking steps to know yourself better. Knowing your strengths and weaknesses, triggers, filters, and thought patterns are the first step toward becoming a calm, mindful, confident teen.

It can be hard to be aware of how quickly negative emotions and thoughts can flood your mind. Before you know it, you may be in the midst of a panic attack, in a rage, or simply overwhelmed by all that is going on around you.

In this book, I have shared the powerful ability that CBT has to put you back in the driver's seat. You now know that situations themselves aren't good or bad; it's how you perceive them and choose to behave that makes all the difference.

You also know that you are not helpless against thoughts, beliefs, or emotions. You may have held on to negative beliefs almost all your life. You may have picked these beliefs up through family patterns or your experiences at school.

I have shown, however, that if, when a tense situation arises, you take time to understand how your thoughts are leading to emotions that result in harmful behaviors, you can turn things around completely. You can reframe your thoughts, challenge negative beliefs, and experiment with new behaviors that enable you to achieve your goals and stop being a slave to your thoughts and emotions.

This book has provided you with a myriad of exercises that require just a few minutes to complete but can help you see situations that once made you feel powerless in a whole new light.

Recognizing harmful habits like using cognitive distortions (or negative filters) is also essential. It is amazing how these filters can confuse us into seeing reality based on preconceived ideas and beliefs instead of facts. CBT is also helpful in encouraging you to base your actions on evidence instead of assumptions.

The book has also provided you with exercises to deal with some of the specific challenges that many teens battle. These include anxiety, depression, anger management, and social anxiety.

This book is not intended to replace therapy for serious mental conditions or symptoms but rather to help you understand the link between your thoughts, emotions, beliefs, and behaviors. By changing just one of these factors, you can reap big benefits in all the other factors. For instance, if you experiment with a new behavior, you may find that you think about a situation in a much more positive light.

Finally, we ended with two approaches that are perfectly compatible with CBT: NLP and DBT. The latter is actually a type of CBT with a big focus on mindfulness. NLP can be a great ally, especially if you enjoy visualizing. It encourages you to reduce the impact problems have and to strengthen the influence that positive goals and thoughts have on your mindset.

I hope you are motivated to start your journey of growth with CBT. Knowing yourself and understanding that you can be your biggest ally or enemy are skills that will stand you in good stead for the rest of your life. Remember that this will be a lifelong journey. As stated by Jiddu Krishnamurti, *"The more you know yourself, the more clarity there is. Self-knowledge has no end—you don't come to an achievement, you don't come to a conclusion. It is an endless river."*

THANKS FOR READING MY BOOK!

I sincerely hope you enjoyed this book, and that you will benefit from what was discussed.

I would be incredibly grateful if you could take a few seconds to leave me an honest review or a star-rating on Amazon. (A star-rating only takes a couple of clicks).

Your review helps other young adults discover this book, and may also help them on their life journey. It will also be good Karma for you.

Scan this code to leave a review.

SOMETHING FOR YOU!

Get your printable workbook today!

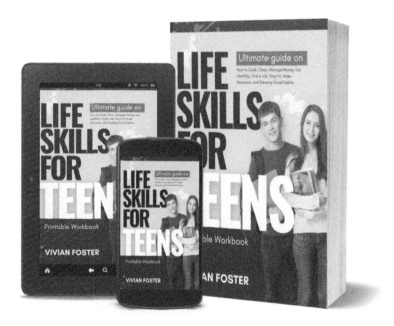

Scan this code to download.

References

Ackerman, C. E. (2017, June 26). *17 therapy worksheets for teens, adults, and couples (+PDFs)*. Positive Psychology. https://positivepsychology.com/therapy-worksheets/

Ackerman, C. E. (2017, September 29). *Cognitive distortions*. Positive Psychology. https://positivepsychology.com/cognitive-distortions/

Adults: A Practice Brief. UNC Frank Porter Graham Child Development Institute. https://fpg.unc.edu/sites/fpg.unc.edu/files/resources/reports-and-policy-briefs/Promoting%20Self-Regulation%20in%20Adolescents%20and%20Young%20Adults.pdf

Alcoholics Anonymous. (n.d.). *Origin of the serenity prayer: A historical paper*. https://www.aa.org/sites/default/files/literature/assets/smf-129_en.pdf

Anger Alternatives. (n.d.). *"Anger is a signal and one worth listening to!" — Dr. Harriet Lerner*. https://www.anger.org/anger-management/anger-is-a-signal-and-one-worth-listening-to-dr-harriet-lerner.html

Aswell, S. (2020, August 20). *I use this 5-minute therapy technique every day for my anxiety*. Healthline. https://www.healthline.com/health/mental-health/self-talk-exercises

Bailey, E. (2014, April 22). *DIY exposure therapy: Social situations*. Health Central. https://www.healthcentral.com/article/diy-exposure-therapy-social-situations

Berashat M, A., & Naghipoor, M. (2019, November 4). Paradox therapy for the treatment of social anxiety disorder: A case study. *Journal of Systems and Integrative Neuroscience, 6*, 1-5. https://doi.org/15761/JSIN.1000213

Boogard, K. (2021, December 26). *How to write SMART goals.* Atlassian. https://www.atlassian.com/blog/productivity/how-to-write-smart-goals#:~:text=What%20are%20SMART%20goals%3F,within%20a%20certain%20time%20frame.

Branch, R., & Wilson, R. (2021, June 25). *Core beliefs and cognitive behavioral therapy.* Dummies. https://www.dummies.com/article/body-mind-spirit/emotional-health-psychology/psychology/cognitive-behavioral-therapy/core-beliefs-and-cognitive-behavioural-therapy-267188/

Central Washington University. (n.d.). *Proactive vs reactive language.* https://www.cwu.edu/learning-commons/sites/cts.cwu.edu.academic-success/files/documents/Proactive%20vs%20Reactive%20Language%20LC.pdf

Chadwick, P., Birchwood, M., & Trower, P. (1996) *Cognitive therapy for delusions, voices and paranoia.* Wiley Series in Clinical Psychology. John Wiley and Sons.

Cherry, K. (2022, September 1). *How to be more positive.* Verywell Mind. https://www.verywellmind.com/how-to-be-more-positive-6499974

Child Development Center. (n.d.). *What is cognitive behavioral therapy?* https://www.cdchk.org/parent-tips/enhancing-emotional-regulation-with-cbt/#:~:text=Cognitive%20Behavioural%20Therapy%20(CBT)%20is,linked%20and%20affect%20each%20other

Child Welfare League of America. (n.d.). *Teens: 70 percent see anxiety and depression as major problem.* https://www.cwla.org/teens-70-percent-see-anxiety-and-depression-as-major-problem/

Chris. (n.d.). *The NLP meta model.* Insights NLP. https://insightsnlp.com/the-nlp-meta-model/

Cleveland Clinic. (20189, October 3). *How to turn your negative thinking around.* https://health.clevelandclinic.org/turn-around-negative-thinking/#:~:text=A%3A%20Negative%20thinking%20makes%20you,%2Dcompulsive%20disorder%20(OCD)

Cleveland Clinic. (2022, March 24). *9 ways to calm your anxiety and anxious thoughts*. https://health.clevelandclinic.org/is-anxiety-ruling-your-life-try-9-ways-to-keep-it-at-bay/

Cuncic, A. (2021, September 1). *Therapy for social anxiety disorder*. Verywell Mind. https://www.verywellmind.com/how-is-cbt-used-to-treat-sad-3024945#:~:text=Cognitive%20behavioral%20therapy%20is%20one,you%20experience%20in%20social%20situations.

Cuncic, A. (2022, January 27). *How to develop and practice self-regulation*. Verywell Mind. https://www.verywellmind.com/how-you-can-practice-self-regulation-4163536

Discovery Mood. (n.d.). *Depression symptoms in teens: Why today's teens are more depressed than ever*. https://discoverymood.com/blog/todays-teens-depressed-ever/

Dr. Emma Black. (2022, April 11). *Personality traits can be positive and negative*. https://townsvillepsychologist.com.au/personality-traits-can-be-positive-and-negative/

Eden Counseling. (n.d.). *Emotional regulation group 4 handouts*. https://www.edencounseling.com/resources/dbt-emotional-regulation-group-4-handouts.pdf

Family Therapy Institute of Santa Barbara. (n.d.). *Assertiveness worksheets*. https://ftisb.org/wp-content/uploads/2021/01/Assertiveness-Worksheets.pdf

Ferrari M., Yap, K., Scott, N., Einstein, D. A., & Ciarrochi, J. (2018, February 21). Self-compassion moderates the perfectionism and depression link in both adolescence and adulthood. *PLOS ONE, 13*(2). https://doi.org/10.1371/journal.pone.0192022

Finerman, A. (2019, November 19). *The impact of limiting beliefs*. Wharton Magazine. https://magazine.wharton.upenn.edu/digital/the-impact-of-limiting-beliefs/

Fursland, A., Raykos, B., & Steele, A. (2009). *Perfectionism in Perspective.* Centre for Clinical Interventions. https://www.cci.health.wa.gov.au/-/media/CCI/Consumer-Modules/Perfectionism-in-Perspective/Perfectionism-in-Perspective---07---Adjusting-unhelpful-rules-and-assumptions.pdf

Goel, P. (2022, September 16). *Wonder why your child is full of anger? Check these 5 likely reasons.* Health Shots. https://www.healthshots.com/preventive-care/family-care/mental-health-disorders-5-causes-of-anger-issues-in-children/

Gotter, A. (2019, April 22). *8 breathing exercises to try when you feel anxious.* Healthline. https://www.healthline.com/health/breathing-exercises-for-anxiety

Greene, P. (2020, July 27). *DBT: Improve the moment – How to make crises bearable.* Manhattan CBT. https://www.manhattancbt.com/archives/1699/dbt-improve-the-moment/

Gupta, S. (2021, July 29). *What is anger management therapy?* Verywell Mind. https://www.verywellmind.com/anger-management-therapy-definition-techniques-and-efficacy-5192566#:~:text=Cognitive%20Behavioral%20Therapy%20(CBT)%3A,cal mer%20and%20more%20in%20control

Healthline. (2022, September 14). *The 15 best essential oils for anxiety.* https://www.healthline.com/health/anxiety/essential-oils-for-anxiety#:~:text=According%20to%20a%202006%20study,undiluted%20an d%20100%20percent%20pure.

Hill, D. (2016, July 18). *Study finds making art can reduce your stress (No matter how skilled you are).* LifeHack. https://www.lifehack.org/428020/study-finds-making-art-can-reduce-your-stress-no-matter-how-skilled-you-are

HuddleIQ. (n.d.). *A six-step plan for problem solving.* https://huddleiq.com/a-six-step-plan-for-problem-solving/

Hurley, K. (2022, July 14). *What is resilience? Your guide to facing life's challenges, adversities, and crises.* Everyday Health. https://www.everydayhealth.com/wellness/resilience/

Ineffable Living. (2022, October 4). *Top 14 CBT exercise for anger management (+ free anger management sheets)*. https://ineffableliving.com/manage-your-anger/#11-top-14-cbt-exercise-for-anger-management

Jacobson, R. (n.d.). *Teens and anger: How parents can model healthy coping skills*. Child Mind Institute. https://childmind.org/article/teens-and-anger/

Kotz, D. (2012, July 3). *Nearly 1 in 12 teens has anger disorder, Harvard study finds*. Boston.com. https://www.boston.com/uncategorized/noprimarytagmatch/2012/07/03/nearly-1-in-12-teens-has-anger-disorder-harvard-study-finds/

Lim, L., Saulsman, L., & Nathan, P. (2005). *Improving self-esteem*. Centre for Clinical Interventions. https://www.cci.health.wa.gov.au/-/media/CCI/Consumer-Modules/Improving-Self-Esteem/Improving-Self-Esteem---08---Developing-Balanced-Core-Beliefs.pdf

Madel. (2023, January 29). *6 ideas for self-care journaling (How to journal for self-care)*. Tracking Happiness. https://www.trackinghappiness.com/how-to-self-care-journal/

Martins Hervington. (2000, September 4). *How to develop your emotional intelligence with NLP*. https://martinshervington.com/nlp/

Mayo Clinic. (n.d.). *Complicated grief*. https://www.mayoclinic.org/diseases-conditions/complicated-grief/symptoms-causes/syc-20360374

Mind Tools. (n.d.). *Dealing with guilt*. https://www.mindtools.com/ajkye4s/dealing-with-guilt

Moore, C. (2019, March 4). *Positive daily affirmations: Is there science behind it?* Positive Psychology. https://positivepsychology.com/daily-affirmations/#science

Morin, A. (2019, November 8). *How to teach time management skills to teens*. VeryWell Family. https://www.verywellfamily.com/teaching-time-management-skills-to-teens-2608794

Murray, D. W. & Rosanbalm, K. (2017). *Promoting Self-Regulation in Adolescents and Young.* UNC Frank Porter Graham Child Development Institute. *https://fpg.unc.edu/sites/fpg.unc.edu/files/resources/reports-and-policy-briefs/Promoting%20Self-Regulation%20in%20Adolescents%20and%20Young%20Adults.pdf*

National Sleep Foundation. (2020, October 28). *What is sleep quality?* https://www.thensf.org/what-is-sleep-quality/#:~:text=Sleep%20quality%20is%20the%20measurement,the%20sleep%20you%20are%20getting

National Social Anxiety Center. (n.d.). *Head-held-high assertion.* https://nationalsocialanxietycenter.com/wp-content/uploads/2022/12/Part-5-Handouts.pdf

Newport Academy. (2022, September 30). *The effects of teenage hormones on adolescent emotions.* https://www.newportacademy.com/resources/empowering-teens/teenage-hormones-and-sexuality/#:~:text=Teen%20hormones%20affect%20teenagers%27%20moods,think%20about%20dating%20and%20sex

NHS. (n.d.). *How it works – Cognitive behavioural therapy.* https://www.nhs.uk/mental-health/talking-therapies-medicine-treatments/talking-therapies-and-counselling/cognitive-behavioural-therapy-cbt/how-it-works/#:~:text=CBT%20aims%20to%20stop%20negative,improve%20the%20way%20you%20feel

NLP Essential Guide. (n.d.). *2-7 swish examples: Size, brightness, distance.* https://nlpessentialguide.com/nlp-swish-pattern/

Northeastern Ohio Universities Colleges of Medicine and Pharmacy. (n.d.). *Twenty questions to help challenge negative thoughts.* https://www.mcgill.ca/counselling/files/counselling/20_questions_to_challenge_negative_thoughts_0.pdf

Optimist Minds. (n.d.). *Emotional regulation worksheet-Emotional regulation.* https://optimistminds.com/emotional-regulation-worksheets/

Oxford Clinical Psychology. (n.d.). *Monitoring the three components of social anxiety*. https://global.oup.com/us/companion.websites/fdscontent/uscompanion/us/pdf/treatments/Mng_Social_Anxiety_wrkshts.pdf

Oxford Clinical Psychology. (n.d.). *Pros and cons of working on my social anxiety*. https://global.oup.com/us/companion.websites/fdscontent/uscompanion/us/pdf/treatments/Mng_Social_Anxiety_wrkshts.pdf

Paradigm Treatment. (n.d.). *Dissociative disorder treatment*. https://paradigmtreatment.com/dissociative-disorder/#:~:text=Depersonalization%20Disorder%20%E2%80%93%20This%20subtype%20is,also%20experience%20depression%20and%20anxiety

Polaris Teen Center. (2019, February 27). *Social anxiety in teens: Signs, symptoms, and how to help*. https://polaristeen.com/articles/social-anxiety-in-teens/#:~:text=Social%20anxiety%20disorder%20(SAD)%20affects,health%20disorder%20in%20the%20country

Positive Psychology. (n.d.). *ABC functional analysis worksheet*. https://positive.b-cdn.net/wp-content/uploads/2020/09/ABC-Functional-Analysis-Worksheet.pdf

Positive Psychology. (n.d.). *Assertive communication worksheets*. https://positivepsychology.com/assertive-communication-worksheets/#worksheets

Positive Psychology. (n.d.). *Behavior contract*. https://positive.b-cdn.net/wp-content/uploads/2021/03/Behavior-Contract.pdf

Positive Psychology. (n.d.). *Guilt and shame emotions that drive depression*. https://positive.b-cdn.net/wp-content/uploads/2021/04/Guilt-and-Shame-Emotions-That-Drive-Depression.pdf

Positive Psychology. (n.d.). *Rights of assertiveness*. https://positive.b-cdn.net/wp-content/uploads/2020/11/Rights-of-Assertiveness.pdf

Positive Psychology. (n.d.). *Table of common core beliefs*. https://positive.b-cdn.net/wp-content/uploads/2020/06/Table-of-Common-Core-Beliefs.pdf

Psychology Tools. (n.d.). *Behavioral experiment.*
https://www.psychologytools.com/resource/behavioral-experiment/

Psychology Tools. (n.d.). *Fight or flight response.*
https://www.psychologytools.com/resource/fight-or-flight-
response/#:~:text=The%20fight%20or%20flight%20response,body%20to
%20fight%20or%20flee

Pulcu, E., Zahn, R., & Elliott, R. (2013, June 3). The role of self-blaming
moral emotions in major depression and their impact on social-
economical decision making. *Frontiers in Psychology, 4.*
https://doi.org/10.3389/fpsyg.2013.00310

Raising Children. (n.d.). *Brain development in pre-teens and teenagers.*
https://raisingchildren.net.au/pre-teens/development/understanding-your-
pre-teen/brain-development-teens

Resolve. (n.d.). *Proactive vs reactive responding.*
https://www.kcresolve.com/blog/proactive-versus-reactive-
responding#:~:text=BEing%20reactive%20means%20blaming%20others,r
esentful%2C%20insecure%2C%20or%20angry

Sattin, N. (2015, November 10). *How to turn your anger into a force for
good with Harriet Lerner.* Neil Sattin.
https://www.neilsattin.com/blog/2015/11/12-how-to-turn-your-anger-
into-a-force-for-good-with-harriet-lerner/

Schaffner, A. K. (2020, June 26). *Core beliefs: 12 worksheets to challenge
negative beliefs.* Positive Psychology.
https://positivepsychology.com/core-beliefs-worksheets/

Selva, J. (2018, March 8). *What is Albert Ellis' ABC model in CBT theory?
(Incl. PDF).* Positive Psychology. https://positivepsychology.com/albert-
ellis-abc-model-rebt-cbt/

Silber, D. (2021, September 14). *The real effects of negative thinking.*
LinkedIn. https://www.linkedin.com/pulse/real-effects-negative-thinking-
dr-debi-silber/

Silva Casabianca, S. (2022, January 11). *15 cognitive distortions to blame for
negative thinking.* Positive Psychology.
https://positivepsychology.com/cognitive-distortions/

Six Seconds. (n.d.). *Plutchik's wheel of emotions. Exploring the emotion wheel.* https://www.6seconds.org/2022/03/13/plutchik-wheel-emotions/

Skyland Trail. (2017, August 27). *4 differences between CBT and DBT and how to tell which is right for you.* https://www.skylandtrail.org/4-differences-between-cbt-and-dbt-and-how-to-tell-which-is-right-for-you/#:~:text=CBT%20seeks%20to%20give%20patients,potentially%20destructive%20or%20harmful%20behaviors.

Smith, K. (2022, October 21). *6 common triggers of teen stress.* Pyscom. https://www.psycom.net/common-triggers-teen-stress

Spring Psychology. (2022, June 21). *"Safe place" relaxation exercise.* https://www.springpsychology.co.uk/post/safe-place-relaxation-exercise

Stade, L. (2019, November 29). *Kids are hardwired to be negative…you can change that!* Linda Stade. https://lindastade.com/overcoming-negativity-children/

Sunrise. *DEAR MAN DBT skill: The most effective way to make a request.* https://sunrisertc.com/dear-man/

The American Institute of Stress. (n.d.). *Stress in teens.* https://www.stress.org/teens

Therapist Aid. (n.d.). *Activity list.* https://www.therapistaid.com/worksheets/activity-list

Therapist Aid. (n.d.). Anger Iceberg. https://www.therapistaid.com/therapy-worksheet/anger-iceberg/anger/none

Therapist Aid. (n.d.). *Challenging negative thoughts.* https://www.therapistaid.com/therapy-worksheet/challenging-negative-thoughts

Therapist Aid. (n.d.). *Coping skills: Anger.* https://www.therapistaid.com/worksheets/coping-skills-anger

Therapist Aid. (n.d.). *Coping skills: Depression.* https://www.therapistaid.com/worksheets/coping-skills-depression

Therapist Aid. (n.d.). *Cost/benefit analysis.* https://www.therapistaid.com/worksheets/cost-benefit-analysis

Therapist Aid. (n.d.). *Creating an exposure hierarchy.*
https://www.therapistaid.com/worksheets/creating-an-exposure-hierarchy

Therapist Aid. (n.d.). *DBT skill: ACCEPTS.*
https://www.therapistaid.com/therapy-worksheet/dbt-accepts

Therapist Aid. (n.d.). *Emotional regulation skills.*
https://www.therapistaid.com/worksheets/dbt-emotion-regulation-skills

Therapist Aid. (n.d.). *Grounding techniques.*
https://www.therapistaid.com/therapy-article/grounding-techniques-article

Therapist Aid. (n.d.). *Protective Factors.*
https://www.therapistaid.com/therapy-worksheet/protective-factors/depression/none

Therapist Aid. (n.d.). *Putting thoughts on trial.*
https://www.therapistaid.com/therapy-worksheet/putting-thoughts-on-trial

Therapist Aid. (n.d.). *RAIN mindfulness exercise.*
https://www.therapistaid.com/worksheets/rain-mindfulness-technique

Therapist Aid. (n.d.). *Trick or treat.*
https://www.livingcbt.com/forms/Free%20Self%20Help/trick_or_treat.pdf

Therapist Aid. (n.d.). *Triggers.* https://www.therapistaid.com/therapy-worksheet/exposure-hierarchy#:~:text=Exposure%20or%20fear%20hierarchies%20are,anxiety%20disorder%2C%20and%20specific%20phobias.

Therapist Aid. (n.d.). *Weekly schedule for behavioral activation.*
https://www.therapistaid.com/worksheets/schedule-behavioral-activation

Therapist Aid. (n.d.). *When is anger a problem?*
https://www.therapistaid.com/worksheets/when-is-anger-a-problem

Therapist Aid. (n.d.). *Worry coping cards.*
https://www.therapistaid.com/worksheets/worry-coping-cards

Therapist Aid. (n.d.). *Worry exploration questions.*
https://www.therapistaid.com/therapy-worksheet/worry-exploration-questions

Thompson, S., & Thompson, N. (2018). *The Critically Reflective Practitioner.*
Bloomsbury Publishing.

University of Washington. (n.d.). *Feeling pattern.*
https://depts.washington.edu/uwhatc/PDF/TF-%20CBT/pages/5%20CBT%20for%20Anxiety/anxietyPATTERN%20EXERCISE.pdf

University of Washington. (n.d.). *Self-talk.*
https://depts.washington.edu/uwhatc/PDF/TF-%20CBT/pages/5%20CBT%20for%20Anxiety/Negative%20Self-Talk%202.pdf

University of Washington. (n.d.). *Worry time.*
https://depts.washington.edu/uwhatc/PDF/TF-%20CBT/pages/5%20CBT%20for%20Anxiety/Worry%20Time%20Log.pdf

Valenti, L. (2019, May 30). *5 young celebrities who have opened up about their mental health in 2019.* Vogue.
https://www.vogue.com/article/celebrity-mental-health-struggles-justin-bieber-sophie-turner-billie-eilish

Wooll, M. (2020, July 19). *Don't let limiting beliefs hold you back. Learn to overcome yours.* BetterUp. https://www.betterup.com/blog/what-are-limiting-beliefs#:~:text=A%20limiting%20belief%20is%20a,how%20you%20interact%20with%20people.

Wyatt, N. (n.d.). *What is NLP? – Is NLP different to CBT?* The Billericay Counsellor. https://thebillericaycounsellor.com/what-is-nlp-is-nlp-different-to-cbt/#:~:text=CBT%20and%20NLP%20are%20actually,used%20by%20Counsellors%20and%20Hypnotherapists

Made in the USA
Las Vegas, NV
20 October 2023

79305933R00125